WeightWatchers®

COOK SMART family food

Healthy, great-tasting recipes all the family will love

SIMON &
SCHUSTER

London • New York • Sydney • Toronto

First published in Great Britain by Simon & Schuster UK Ltd, 2009
A CBS Company

Weight Watchers Publications Team: Jane Griffiths, Donna Watts, Nina McKerlie and Eileen Thornton

Photography by Steve Baxter, Iain Bagwell and Steve Lee
Design and typesetting by Jane Norman
Printed and bound in China

A CIP catalogue for this book is available from the British Library

ISBN 978-1-84737-390-8

1 3 5 7 9 10 8 6 4 2

Pictured on the front cover: Individual Roasted Vegetable Pizzas page 50, Overnight Muesli page 24,
Roast Chicken with Rosemary and Lemon Potatoes page 72, Summer Puddings page 148
Pictured on the back cover: Bold Berry Smoothie page 31, Spring Rolls page 62, Montezuma Ice Cream with Marshmallows page 126,
Fruity Chocolate Fridge Cake page 154
Pictured on the introduction: Full English Breakfast, page 10, Seafood Chowder page 38, Prawn and Chilli Tagliatelle page 78,
Lemon and Ginger Tart page 144

 POINTS® value logo: You'll find this easy to read **POINTS** value logo on every recipe throughout this book. The logo represents the number of
POINTS values per serving each recipe contains. For more information about Weight Watchers and the **POINTS** Plan, call 0845 712 3000.

V This symbol denotes a vegetarian recipe and assumes that, where relevant, free range eggs, vegetarian cheese, vegetarian virtually fat free fromage
frais and vegetarian low fat crème fraîche are used. Virtually fat free fromage frais and low fat crème fraîche may contain traces of gelatine so they
are not always vegetarian. Please check the labels.

✱ This symbol denotes a dish that can be frozen.

Recipe notes
Egg size: Medium, unless otherwise stated.

All fruits and vegetables: Medium size, unless otherwise stated.

Raw eggs: Only the freshest eggs should be used. Pregnant women, the elderly and children should avoid recipes with eggs that are not fully cooked
or raw.

Recipe timings: These are approximate and meant to be guidelines. Please note that the preparation time includes all the steps up to and following the
main cooking time(s).

Low fat polyunsaturated margarine: Use brands such as Flora Light, St Ivel Gold and Benecol Light.

Contents

Introduction

This book is designed for those who want to eat healthily and make sure that their family enjoys good food. It's for people who lead busy lives and don't have a great deal of time to spend in the kitchen, but who do want to eat nutritious tasty meals every day.

As well as delicious recipes, you will find hints and tips throughout the book. Boxes on Eating Wisely, Cooking Basics and Store Cupboard Ideas should all help you to make the most of your time and provide great meals for the family.

There's extra information in the next two pages as well: tips on basic ingredients, as well as a list of useful things to keep in your store cupboard.

About Weight Watchers

For more than 40 years Weight Watchers has been helping people around the world to lose weight using a long term sustainable approach. Weight Watchers successful weight loss system is based on four tried and trusted principles:

- Eating healthily
- Being more active
- Adjusting behaviour to help weight loss
- Getting support in weekly meetings.

Our unique *POINTS* system empowers you to manage your food plan and make wise recipe choices for a healthier, happier you.

Basic Ingredients

Milk

Always use skimmed milk, rather than whole or semi-skimmed, unless otherwise stated in the recipe.

Eggs

Use medium sized eggs, unless otherwise stated in the recipe. Always bring eggs to room temperature before using. A cold egg won't whisk well and the shell will crack if placed in hot water.

Fats and oils

The majority of recipes use low fat cooking spray rather than oil. Low fat cooking spray can be either olive oil or sunflower oil based. Try both and see which you prefer.

Generally, low fat polyunsaturated margarine is used in recipes rather than butter.

Cheese and yogurt

The cheese used in these recipes is low fat Cheddar, low fat soft cheese or virtually fat free fromage frais. Many recipes use yogurt. Always choose either 0% fat Greek yogurt or low fat natural or fruit yogurt. Quark – a very low fat soft cheese made with skimmed milk – is also used. All of these products are easy to find in a supermarket.

Fruit and vegetables

Make sure your family eats plenty of fruit and vegetables, preferably at least five portions a day. Try putting a fruit snack in lunchboxes and always offer your family at least one vegetable with the main meal. Filling up on fruit and vegetables will also stop you from feeling hungry, so you are less likely to snack on fatty and sugary foods.

There are plenty of vegetarian recipes in the book, including healthy salads and soups, as well as suggestions for vegetable accompaniments.

Planning Ahead

When you're going around the supermarket it is tempting to pick up foods you like and put them in your trolley without thinking about how you will use them. So, a good plan is to decide what dishes you want to cook before you go shopping, check your store cupboard ingredients and make a list of what you need. You'll save time by not drifting aimlessly around the supermarket picking up what you fancy. You might even have time for a cup of tea or coffee.

Store Cupboard Suggestions

artificial sweetener

baking powder

bay leaves

bicarbonate of soda

black pepper

borlotti beans, canned

cannellini beans, canned

cereal (bran and muesli)

chick peas, canned

chilli (flakes and powder)

chocolate (70%+)

cloves

cocoa powder

coffee, instant

condensed milk, light

cornflour

corn oil

couscous

curry powder

custard, low fat

flour (plain, brown, wholemeal and self raising)

fish sauce, Thai

fruit, canned

fruit, dried (sultanas, apricots, blueberries, etc.)

garlic cloves

gelatine

gravy granules

herbs, dried (mixed, oregano, thyme, etc.)

honey

jam, reduced sugar

kidney beans

lemons

lentils, canned

low fat cooking spray

low fat peanut butter

mayonnaise, extra light

marmalade, reduced sugar

mushrooms, dried

mustard (English and wholegrain)

noodles (rice and egg)

nuts

oil (olive and sunflower)

passata

pasta

pastry, filo

peppercorns

pizza bases

polenta (cornmeal)

porridge oats

rice (basmati, brown and risotto)

salt (sea salt or low sodium)

seeds (caraway, fennel, pumpkin and sesame)

semolina

spices, ground (cinnamon, nutmeg, ginger, paprika, cayenne pepper, coriander, cumin, etc.)

soy sauce, light

stock cubes (vegetable, chicken and beef)

sugar (caster, icing, demerara and muscovado)

sugar free jelly

sweetcorn, canned or frozen

tomato ketchup

tomato purée

tomatoes, canned

tuna, canned in brine or in spring water

vanilla essence

vinegar (balsamic, rice and white wine)

Breakfasts and Brunches

Probably the most important meal of the day, breakfast can be anything from a Bold Berry Smoothie to a Big Fruit Breakfast. Or try a more leisurely weekend affair such as Eggs Florentine or Kedgeree. Choose from a wide range of healthy options that will set you up for the day and will also give the whole family an energy boost.

Start the day the right way with a healthy breakfast

Full English Breakfast

This recipe shows you how easy it is to enjoy a full English breakfast while you are trying to lose weight.

Serves 4

200 g (7 oz) turkey rashers
4 ripe tomatoes, sliced in half crossways
4 slices medium wholemeal bread
low fat cooking spray
200 g (7 oz) mushrooms, sliced
2 large lemon wedges
4 eggs
30 g (1¼ oz) low fat spread
salt and freshly ground black pepper

4 *POINTS* values per serving
15½ *POINTS* values per recipe

240 calories per serving

Takes **20 minutes**

not recommended

1 Preheat the grill and place the turkey rashers and tomatoes, cut side up and seasoned, on the grill pan. Grill for 3–4 minutes then turn the turkey rashers over and grill again for 2 minutes, until golden and crispy.

2 Meanwhile, warm four serving plates, toast the bread and heat a non stick frying pan. Spray with the low fat cooking spray and then add the mushrooms. Stir fry for 3–4 minutes on a high heat until softened, then season, squeeze over the lemon and remove from the heat.

3 Tip the mushrooms on to the serving plates and keep warm. Return the frying pan to a low heat. Spray again with the cooking spray and then carefully break in the eggs. Fry over a gentle heat until they are cooked how you like them.

4 Meanwhile spread the toast with the spread and slice in half, then place on the serving plates with the mushrooms. Add the cooked turkey rashers, tomatoes and eggs and serve immediately.

Eat wisely Low fat cooking spray is an absolute must for eating the Weight Watchers way. It works as a substitute for oil, but only has one calorie per spray. You can use it for frying, roasting, browning and grilling. You can get different varieties, with either sunflower or olive oil bases, depending on your preference.

Eggs Florentine

A classic brunch dish that's been adapted here for a healthier lifestyle.

Serves 4

350 g (12 oz) baby spinach leaves, washed
a couple of pinches of fresh nutmeg
1 tablespoon vinegar (any type)
4 eggs
2 muffins, sliced in half
4 tablespoons fat free fromage frais
4 pinches of paprika
salt and freshly ground black pepper

3 *POINTS* values per serving
11 *POINTS* values per recipe

C 189 calories per serving

Takes 10 minutes

V

* not recommended

1 Place the wet spinach in a lidded saucepan with seasoning and the nutmeg. Cover and cook on a low heat, stirring occasionally, for 3–4 minutes until wilted. Keep warm.

2 Heat a medium saucepan of water to a rolling boil and add the vinegar. One at a time, break the eggs into a cup and gently lower them from the cup into the boiling water. Poach the eggs for 2–3 minutes until the white is firm, but the yolk still runny (or how you prefer). Remove with a slotted spoon.

3 Meanwhile toast the muffins and place on plates with a pile of the cooked spinach on each one. Make a slight hollow in the top of the spinach and carefully spoon in the poached eggs. Spoon the fromage frais over the eggs and dust with paprika to serve.

Eat wisely Opt for healthy cooking methods such as steaming, grilling or poaching rather than frying. The flavour will be just as good, but you won't need to use lots of oil or butter and any excess fat will drain away.

Bacon and Egg Bubble and Squeak

If you've got leftover vegetables, don't throw them out. They're easily added to soup or, even better, they can be made into this quick and tasty breakfast treat.

Serves 4

350 g (12 oz) cooked boiled potatoes, chopped roughly
200 g (7 oz) cooked cabbage, shredded
200 g (7 oz) cooked carrots, chopped
50 g (1¾ oz) spring onions, chopped finely
4 tablespoons freshly chopped parsley
4 eggs, beaten
2 tablespoons skimmed milk
low fat cooking spray
100 g (3½ oz) lean bacon rashers, preferably smoked, snipped into small pieces
salt and freshly ground black pepper

4 **POINTS** values per serving
15½ **POINTS** values per recipe

C 231 calories per serving

Takes **35 minutes**

✳ not recommended

1 Put the potatoes, cabbage and carrots into a bowl and mix together. Stir in the spring onions, some seasoning and all but 1 tablespoon of the parsley.

2 In a separate bowl, mix the eggs with the milk and season. Set aside.

3 Spray a non stick frying pan with low fat cooking spray and heat to medium hot. Fry the bacon pieces for 2–3 minutes or until cooked, and then add them to the potato mixture. Turn the heat down to medium and remove the pan from the hob.

4 Use your hands to squeeze the mixture together and form eight balls. Spray the pan with a little more cooking spray and put the balls in the frying pan. Gently squash down on them to make little pattie shapes and return the pan to the heat. Fry them for 5 minutes on each side or until they are brown and heated right through. You may have to do this in batches. Remove them and put two patties on each of four warm plates.

5 Reduce the temperature of the pan, spray it again with cooking spray and pour the eggs into the frying pan, stirring continuously. The eggs will cook in seconds, so be ready to remove the pan from the heat and top the patties with the eggs. Garnish with the remaining parsley and serve immediately.

Vegetarian variation Omit the bacon for a vegetarian bubble and squeak, reducing the **POINTS** values to 2½ per serving.

Potato Pancakes with Turkey Rashers and Tomatoes

A tempting treat for a weekend brunch, these potato pancakes are also a healthy alternative to hash browns.

Serves 4

2 eggs, beaten
30 g (1¼ oz) self raising flour
450 g (1 lb) baking potatoes, peeled
low fat cooking spray
8 turkey rashers
4 tomatoes, halved
salt and freshly ground black pepper

3 *POINTS* values per serving
12 *POINTS* values per recipe

221 calories per serving

Takes 20 minutes

* not recommended

1 Preheat the grill.

2 Mix the eggs and flour together to form a batter.

3 Coarsely grate the potatoes then squeeze out the excess moisture. Stir into the batter and season generously.

4 Lightly coat a lidded non stick frying pan with low fat cooking spray then spoon half the potato mixture into the pan as four separate pancakes. Cook over a medium heat for 3 minutes each side until golden brown.

5 Reduce the heat, cover the pan and cook for 2 minutes more to cook the pancakes through. Remove and keep warm. Repeat with the other half of the potato mixture.

6 Meanwhile, grill the turkey rashers and halved tomatoes for about 5 minutes, or until cooked to your liking. Serve with the potato pancakes.

Store cupboard ideas Always keep some pepper in the cupboard as it adds a final, distinctive flavour to your dishes. You can buy pepper whole, cracked or ground – but try to buy whole peppercorns and then pop them in a pepper mill for freshly ground pepper any time. Freshly ground pepper is more pungent than pre-ground and can be stored for up to a year.

Sweetcorn Fritters

This cooked breakfast is a taste of America – a delicious, different way to start the day.

Serves 4

low fat cooking spray
4 eggs, beaten
½ red onion, diced finely
½ teaspoon mustard powder (optional)
200 g (7 oz) sweetcorn
2 tablespoons freshly chopped parsley or
   coriander, plus extra to garnish
2 beef tomatoes, each sliced into at least
   four slices
salt and freshly ground black pepper

2 *POINTS* values per serving
7½ *POINTS* values per recipe

C 166 calories per serving

Takes **20 minutes**

V

* not recommended

1 Spray a large non stick frying pan or griddle pan with low fat cooking spray and preheat to a medium hot temperature.

2 Using a fork or a balloon whisk, combine all the ingredients except the tomato slices in a large mixing bowl. Season well. Create a fritter by putting two generous tablespoons of the mixture into the pan. (Stir the mix between each spoonful, or the corn will all sink to the bottom of the bowl). If all the corn is in the middle of the fritter, gently spread the kernels out to its edges.

3 Repeat with another two spoonfuls of mixture at the other side of the pan and cook both fritters for a minute or two, or until the egg has set enough to turn the fritters over. Cook on the other side for a couple of minutes and check both sides are browned. While the fritters are cooking, pop the tomato slices into the pan and heat through on both sides.

4 Cook the fritters in batches, keeping them warm until you have eight cooked fritters. Warm four plates. Serve each fritter topped with a slice of tomato and a sprinkling of fresh herbs.

Variation For bacon lovers, dry fry eight bacon medallions with the eight tomato slices before you start on the main fritters. Keep warm until the fritters are ready and then top each fritter with bacon, a slice of tomato and the herbs, for an additional 3 *POINTS* values per serving.

Kedgeree

This makes an excellent weekend breakfast for the whole family.

Serves 4

200 g (7 oz) long grain rice
2 tablespoons medium curry powder
2 eggs
400 g (14 oz) smoked haddock fillets
300 ml (½ pint) fish or vegetable stock
low fat cooking spray
1 onion, chopped
2 tablespoons freshly chopped parsley
2 tomatoes, each cut into six wedges
salt and freshly ground black pepper

4½ **POINTS** values per serving
17½ **POINTS** values per recipe

C 335 calories per serving

Takes **25 minutes**

* not recommended

1 Put the rice and curry powder in a lidded pan and cover with water. Bring to the boil, cover and simmer for 10 minutes.

2 Meanwhile, hard boil the eggs in simmering water for 8 minutes (see below).

3 Place the haddock and stock in a large lidded frying pan, cover and cook for 6 minutes (until the fish flakes easily).

4 Spray a non stick frying pan with low fat cooking spray and cook the onion until just starting to brown.

5 When the fish is cooked, skin and flake the flesh.

6 When the eggs are cooked, plunge into cold water to cool and then remove the shells. Cut into wedges.

7 When the rice is cooked, drain if necessary and then stir in 1 tablespoon of chopped parsley, the onion and fish. Season to taste.

8 Divide the kedgeree between four warmed serving plates, garnish with wedges of egg and tomato and sprinkle with the remaining parsley. Serve immediately.

Cooking basics For perfect hard boiled eggs: try to always use an egg that is at room temperature, rather than one straight from the fridge. Place the eggs in a small saucepan and add enough cold water to just cover them. Slowly bring the water to simmering point and let the eggs cook for about 8 minutes. Gently take the eggs out of the pan and run cold water over them before allowing them to rest in cold water for a couple of minutes.

Smoked Salmon and Scrambled Eggs

A satisfying start to the day with a luxurious twist. Fresh dill or parsley makes a delicious addition.

Serves 2

4 eggs, beaten
8 tablespoons skimmed milk or soya milk
100 g (3½ oz) smoked salmon pieces,
 chopped if necessary
salt and freshly ground black pepper

1 In a large bowl, mix all the ingredients together.

2 Pour the mixture into a non stick saucepan and, using a wooden spoon, stir over a low heat until the eggs are just firm but not dry.

3 Season to taste and serve immediately.

 4 *POINTS* values per serving
8 *POINTS* values per recipe

C **273 calories** per serving

Takes **5 minutes**

✳ not recommended

Tip You can usually buy smoked salmon offcuts quite cheaply in supermarkets and they are perfect for this recipe, which requires the salmon to be chopped into small pieces.

Breakfast Omelette

Save on the washing up with this one pan version of a cooked breakfast.

Serves 1

low fat cooking spray
80 g (3 oz) button mushrooms, quartered
5 cherry tomatoes, halved
2 eggs
salt and freshly ground black pepper

1 Lightly coat a large non stick frying pan with low fat cooking spray and cook the mushrooms for 2 minutes, then add the tomatoes.

2 Beat the eggs with 4 tablespoons of water and seasoning, then pour into the pan. Tip the pan from side to side to spread the egg around, then cook gently for 3–4 minutes, or until set to your liking. Carefully fold over and serve on a warmed plate.

2½ **POINTS** values per serving
2½ **POINTS** values per recipe

C 196 **calories** per serving

Takes **10 minutes**

V

✱ not recommended

Cinnamon French Toast with Apricots

A sweet version of eggy bread that's wonderful for a lazy weekend breakfast.

Serves 4

1 teaspoon ground cinnamon
4 teaspoons granulated artificial sweetener
4 eggs
4 tablespoons skimmed milk
6 medium slices wholemeal bread
low fat cooking spray

To serve

2 x 410 g can apricot halves in juice, drained
4 heaped tablespoons very low fat plain
  fromage frais

4½ **POINTS** values per serving
17½ **POINTS** values per recipe

C 246 **calories** per serving

Takes **10 minutes**

V

✱ not recommended

1 Mix half the cinnamon with the sugar and set aside.

2 Beat the remaining cinnamon together with the eggs and milk in a shallow dish. Cut the bread into triangles and dip into the egg mixture.

3 Lightly coat a non stick frying pan with low fat cooking spray. Cook the eggy bread in four batches, frying over a medium heat for 1½–2 minutes on each side until golden and crisp.

4 Keep warm while you cook the other batches.

5 Divide the French toast between four plates and sprinkle with the cinnamon sugar. Top with the apricots and fromage frais and serve immediately.

Eat wisely If bread is your downfall, an easy way to control what you eat is by freezing your sliced bread. When you are hungry or want some toast, either pop a couple of frozen slices straight into the toaster (for slightly longer than from fresh) or allow the bread to thaw before eating.

Overnight Muesli

Oats make for a great breakfast as they provide slow-release energy throughout the morning.

Serves 2

60 g (2 oz) porridge oats
1 apple, cored and grated coarsely
250 ml (9 fl oz) skimmed milk

To serve
2 heaped tablespoons 0% fat Greek yogurt
80 g (3 oz) fresh blueberries

 3 POINTS values per serving
6½ POINTS values per recipe

C **200 calories** per serving

Takes **5 minutes** + overnight soaking

V

✳ not recommended

1 Place the oats in a bowl or plastic container, stir in the apple and milk, cover and leave to soak and soften overnight in the fridge.

2 In the morning, top each bowlful with a heaped tablespoon of yogurt and the blueberries.

Store cupboard ideas Replace highly processed breakfast cereals with wholegrain, unsweetened varieties, but better still faze them out and make your own. Vary your breakfast with fruit, porridge oats, eggs and smoothies.

Oaty Pancakes with Blueberries

These delicious cinnamon-flavoured fluffy pancakes make a very special breakfast or delectable dessert.

Serves 4

2 eggs, separated
50 g (1¾ oz) self raising flour
50 g (1¾ oz) porridge oats
1 tablespoon artificial sweetener plus an extra pinch
1 teaspoon ground cinnamon
150 ml (5 fl oz) skimmed milk or soya milk
low fat cooking spray
150 g (5½ oz) fresh blueberries

2½ *POINTS* values per serving
10 *POINTS* values per recipe

C 170 **calories** per serving

Takes **20 minutes**

V

✳ not recommended

1 Whisk the egg whites in a clean, grease-free bowl until stiff. In another large bowl beat together the egg yolks, flour, oats, the pinch of sweetener, cinnamon and milk.

2 Fold the egg whites into the mixture with a large metal spoon, being careful to preserve as much of the volume as possible.

3 Heat a non stick frying pan and spray with the low fat cooking spray. Place tablespoons of the batter in the frying pan to make little oval pancakes approximately 8 cm (3¼ inches) in diameter.

4 Cook for 2–3 minutes until golden and spongy and then turn once, using a palette knife or fish slice, and cook until golden on the other side.

5 When cooked, place them on a plate and wrap in a tea towel. Keep warm while you cook the others (the mixture makes about 16 pancakes).

6 Meanwhile warm the blueberries gently in a small saucepan with 100 ml (3½ fl oz) of water and the tablespoon of sweetener. Stir occasionally until the fruit has broken down.

7 Serve the pancakes warm with the hot blueberry sauce, allowing four pancakes per person.

Banana and Honey Crumpets

Popular with adults and children alike, these crumpets are terrific for breakfast or an after work snack.

Serves 4

8 regular crumpets
60 g (2 oz) low fat soft cheese
2 bananas, sliced
¼ teaspoon mixed spice or cinnamon
2 heaped teaspoons honey

3½ *POINTS* values per serving
14½ *POINTS* values per recipe

C **260 calories** per serving

Takes **5 minutes**

V

✱ not recommended

1 Toast the crumpets under a preheated grill then spread with the soft cheese. Pile the banana slices on top, sprinkle with mixed spice and return to the grill for 1 minute to warm through.

2 Drizzle with the honey and eat straightaway.

Eat wisely Replace cream cheese with low fat soft cheeses. However, always check the pack carefully to make sure that it says low fat soft cheese and not medium fat soft cheese, as sometimes the labelling can be deceptive.

Blueberry Muffins

This recipe can be made using dried blueberries, which can be found in the baking section of supermarkets. These are very convenient to keep in your store cupboard.

Makes 12

200 g (7 oz) plain flour
½ teaspoon bicarbonate of soda
2 teaspoons baking powder
75 g (2¾ oz) caster sugar
a pinch of salt
75 g (2¾ oz) low fat polyunsaturated
   margarine, melted
100 ml (3½ fl oz) low fat natural yogurt
100 ml (3½ fl oz) skimmed milk
1 egg
200 g (7 oz) fresh blueberries

2½ **POINTS** values per serving
29½ **POINTS** values per recipe

C **125 calories** per muffin

Takes **15 minutes** to prepare,
20 minutes to bake

V

✱ not recommended

1 Preheat the oven to Gas Mark 6/200°C/fan oven 180°C. Line a Yorkshire pudding tin or muffin tray with 12 muffin or cup cake cases.

2 Combine all the dry ingredients in a bowl. In another bowl mix the melted margarine, yogurt, milk and egg together.

3 Pour the wet ingredients into the dry and combine very gently so you don't over-work the mixture.

4 Gently stir in the blueberries, again keeping the mixing to a minimum, then quickly spoon into the muffin cases. Bake for 20 minutes, until risen and golden on top.

5 Transfer to a wire rack and cool or eat warm.

Tip These muffins keep well for up to 3 days stored in an airtight container.

Variation Substitute the fresh blueberries with dried blueberries; just soak for 10 minutes in hot water. The **POINTS** values per serving will remain the same.

Cinnamon and Apple Muffins

These light and healthy muffins can be made in just 30 minutes. They are perfect for breakfast, especially if you are on the go.

Makes 12

1 egg
75 g (2¾ oz) low fat polyunsaturated margarine, melted
125 ml (4½ fl oz) low fat plain yogurt
100 ml (3½ fl oz) apple juice
3 tablespoons clear honey, warmed
2 large dessert apples, peeled, cored and grated
200 g (7 oz) plain flour
2 teaspoons baking powder
½ teaspoon bicarbonate of soda
a pinch of salt
1 teaspoon ground cinnamon

1 Preheat the oven to Gas Mark 6/200°C/fan oven 180°C. Line a Yorkshire pudding tin or muffin tray with 12 muffin cases.

2 In a large measuring jug beat together the egg, margarine, yogurt, apple juice, honey and grated apple. Mix all the dry ingredients together in a large bowl. Add the wet ingredients to the dry and gently but quickly mix together, then spoon into the muffin cases.

3 Bake for 20 minutes or until risen and the centres spring back when gently pressed. Place on a wire rack to cool and store in an airtight container for up to 3 days.

2 POINTS values per serving
25 POINTS values per recipe

C **115 calories** per muffin

 Takes **15 minutes** to prepare, **20 minutes** to bake + cooling

V

✻ not recommended

Tip Use dessert apples (such as Cox, Gala or Spartan) for the best results.

Bold Berry Smoothie

Smoothies can be a tasty way of helping towards the recommended five portions of fruit and vegetables in your diet every day.

Serves 2

2 small ripe bananas
300 g (10½ oz) frozen mixed summer fruits
200 g (7 oz) very low fat plain yogurt

1 Blend all the ingredients in a liquidiser, adding small quantities of water until you have the consistency you prefer. Drink immediately.

2½ *POINTS* values per serving
5 *POINTS* values per recipe

C **193 calories** per serving

Takes **5 minutes**

V

* recommended

Variation As a dairy-free alternative, use 200 g (7 oz) Galia melon or Cantaloupe melon instead of the banana and yogurt. The *POINTS* values per serving will be 1.

Tip Freeze the smoothie mixture in ice lolly moulds or ice cube trays for delicious, cooling summer treats.

Big Fruit Breakfast

Claimed to be the optimum breakfast, fruit is easy to digest and consequently quick to give you energy. Bio yogurt, too, is great for our digestive systems. Try this breakfast for a few weeks and see how full of vitality you feel.

Serves 2

2 apples, cored and chopped
2 pears, cored and chopped
2 oranges, peeled and sliced
4 plums, stoned and chopped
2 kiwi fruit, peeled and chopped
4 heaped tablespoons of low fat plain bio yogurt

3½ *POINTS* values per serving
6½ *POINTS* values per recipe

C 279 calories per serving

Takes 10 minutes

V

✳ not recommended

1 Toss all the fruit together and divide equally between two bowls.

2 Spoon over the yogurt and eat immediately.

Tip Vary the fruit, try to buy whatever is ripe and in season for the best flavour. Look for local produce as the less a fruit has travelled the fresher it should be – and it will have greater nutritional value. Huge bowls of pick-your-own raspberries and strawberries in the summer are wonderful.

Eat wisely Trying out new combinations is a great way to maintain your motivation when losing weight. Relish everything that you put in your mouth and ask yourself if you're really enjoying it. Cultivate your likes, and experiment with new flavours and textures.

Hot Cross Buns

Makes 16

350 g (12 oz) plain flour
100 g (3½ oz) plain wholemeal flour
25 g (1 oz) fresh yeast (or 15 g/½ oz dried)
½ teaspoon caster sugar
150 ml (5 fl oz) warm water
150 ml (5 fl oz) skimmed milk
1 teaspoon cinnamon
1 teaspoon ground nutmeg
1 teaspoon salt
50 g (1¾ oz) caster sugar
75 g (2¾ oz) currants
50 g (1¾ oz) chopped mixed peel
50 g (1¾ oz) low fat polyunsaturated
  margarine, melted
1 egg, beaten
low fat cooking spray
a little skimmed milk, to glaze

1 Sift half the quantity of each flour into a bowl and make a well in the centre. Blend the yeast with the sugar and a little of the warm water. Leave for 5 minutes in a warm place to froth then add the rest of the water. Pour the yeast mixture and the milk into the well in the flour. Mix well then leave, covered, in a warm place for about 45 minutes until risen to double its size.

2 Meanwhile, sieve the rest of each flour then mix with the spices, salt, caster sugar, currants and peel. Add this mixture to the risen dough with the margarine and egg and mix well with your hands, kneading until smooth. Leave, covered, in a warm place for 1 hour.

3 Turn the risen dough out on to a floured surface and roll or pat it out. Divide into 16 pieces. Shape them into rounds and place well apart on a baking tray that has been sprayed with the cooking spray and then lightly floured.

4 Mark each round with a cross using a sharp knife. Cover and leave either in the fridge overnight ready for baking the next day, or in a warm place for 15 minutes while you preheat the oven to Gas Mark 7/220°C/fan oven 200°C. Brush with a little milk to glaze then bake for 15 minutes. Leave on a wire rack to cool.

2 *POINTS* values per serving
35½ *POINTS* values per recipe

C 149 calories per bun

Takes 30 minutes to prepare + 2–2½ hours rising, 15 minutes to bake

V

 recommended

Tip You can start making these the day before and keep the dough in the fridge to bake in the morning. Remember to remove it from the fridge and leave in a warm place for 30 minutes before baking.

Banana Bread

Everyone loves banana bread, and the sultanas make this version extra fruity.

Makes 12 slices

low fat cooking spray
200 g (7 oz) self raising flour
¼ teaspoon bicarbonate of soda
75 g (2¾ oz) low fat polyunsaturated margarine
75 g (2¾ oz) sugar
1 tablespoon honey, or an extra tablespoon sugar (optional)
2 eggs, beaten
2 ripe bananas, mashed
100 g (3½ oz) sultanas (optional)

1 Preheat the oven to Gas Mark 4/180°C/fan oven 160°C. Spray a 450 g (1 lb) loaf tin with the low fat cooking spray.

2 In a large bowl, sieve the flour and bicarbonate of soda together. In another bowl, cream the margarine, sugar and honey or extra sugar, if using, until light and fluffy. Add the eggs gradually, beating all the time. Gently stir the flour into the creamed mixture, then the mashed bananas and sultanas, if using.

3 Spoon into the prepared tin and bake for about an hour or until just firm. Turn out and cool on a rack.

3½ **POINTS** values per serving
41½ **POINTS** values per recipe

C **159 calories** per slice

Takes **10 minutes** to prepare, **1 hour** to bake + cooling

V

* recommended

Lunches
and Light Bites

It's always good to have a healthy meal in the middle of the day. Try something simple, such as Lemony Chicken Salad, Individual Roasted Vegetable Pizzas or Spring Rolls, or sit down to a more substantial family meal such as Beef Fillet with Horseradish Crust.

Brighten up your lunchtime
by trying something different

Seafood Chowder

Chowders are thick, chunky soups with a creamy base. They are especially popular in America.

Serves 4

low fat cooking spray
1 onion, chopped finely
250 g (9 oz) potatoes, peeled and diced
2 vegetable stock cubes, dissolved in 850 ml
  (1½ pints) boiling water
50 g (1¾ oz) frozen peas
200 g (7 oz) smoked haddock, skinned,
  boned and cut into chunks
100 g (3½ oz) cooked peeled prawns,
  defrosted if frozen
300 ml (10 fl oz) skimmed milk
2 tablespoons freshly chopped parsley
2 tablespoons cornflour, blended with
  5 tablespoons cold water
salt and freshly ground black pepper

2½ **POINTS** values per serving
10 **POINTS** values per recipe

205 **calories** per serving

Takes **15 minutes** to prepare,
20 minutes to cook

* recommended

1 Lightly spray a large lidded saucepan with low fat cooking spray and sauté the onion for 5 minutes, until softened.

2 Add the potatoes and stock to the saucepan. Heat, then cover and simmer gently for about 15 minutes, until the potatoes are tender.

3 Add the peas, haddock, prawns, milk and half the parsley. Cook over a low heat for about 5 minutes, until the fish is opaque.

4 Add the blended cornflour to the saucepan and heat, stirring until thickened. Season, then serve in four warmed bowls, sprinkled with the remaining parsley.

Cooking basics To skin fish: lay the fish fillet skin side down and make a small cut at the tail end, through the flesh to the skin. Place the fish with the tail towards you, then put the blade of the knife under the skin where it has been cut. Holding the skin firmly with your other hand, slide the blade away from you, up to the head of the fish, and then discard the skin.

Chicken Noodle Soup

A bowlful of this tasty low *POINTS* values soup, with its authentic Chinese flavour, is wonderfully filling and enjoyable.

Serves 4

2 chicken stock cubes, dissolved in 850 ml (1½ pints) boiling water
a bunch of spring onions, shredded into fine strips
1 small leek, shredded into fine strips
½ teaspoon Chinese 5 Spice powder
1 teaspoon finely grated fresh root ginger or ¼ teaspoon ground ginger
2 tablespoons light soy sauce
50 g (1¾ oz) thread egg noodles
50 g (1¾ oz) sweetcorn, defrosted if frozen
50 g (1¾ oz) cooked chicken, shredded into fine strips
1 tablespoon cornflour, blended with 3 tablespoons cold water
salt and freshly ground black pepper

1½ *POINTS* values per serving
5½ *POINTS* values per recipe

125 calories per serving

Takes 35 minutes

* recommended

1 Pour the chicken stock into a large lidded saucepan and add the spring onions, leek, 5 Spice powder, ginger and soy sauce. Cover and cook gently for 10 minutes.

2 Add the egg noodles to the saucepan and cook gently for 5 minutes. Now add the sweetcorn and chicken, and cook for 2 minutes more.

3 Mix in the blended cornflour and cook for about 1 minute, stirring, until the soup is thickened and smooth. Season to taste.

4 Ladle the soup into four warmed bowls and serve at once.

Variation Substitute long grain rice for the noodles, adding it with the soy sauce in step 1 so that it has time to cook. The *POINTS* values will remain the same.

Leek and Potato Soup

A perfect winter soup; smooth, subtle, substantial and comforting. It is simple and quick to make and full of goodness.

Serves 4

low fat cooking spray
400 g (14 oz) potatoes, peeled and chopped
   into small pieces
6 large leeks, split in half, washed and
   chopped finely
1.2 litres (2 pints) vegetable stock
300 ml (½ pint) skimmed milk
a pinch of nutmeg
salt and freshly ground black pepper
a bunch of chives, snipped, to garnish
   (optional)

1½ *POINTS* values per serving
5½ *POINTS* values per recipe

175 calories per serving

Takes **15 minutes** to prepare,
20 minutes to cook

V

✳ recommended

1 Heat a large saucepan and spray with the low fat cooking spray. Add the potatoes and stir fry for a few minutes. Add the leeks, stir together and add the stock.

2 Bring to the boil and then simmer, covered, for 20 minutes, until the leeks and potatoes are tender.

3 Add the milk, nutmeg and seasoning and stir through. Serve hot, garnished with snipped chives, if using, and black pepper.

Cooking basics Make soups into an instant snack or lunch by preparing them in advance and freezing. Make a large batch by multiplying the recipe quantities. Then measure the soup out into portions and freeze. When you are ready to eat, simply take it out of the freezer and pop in it the microwave, or gently thaw it on the hob for a quick, wholesome and satisfying filler.

Farmhouse Chicken and Vegetable Broth

Bring back nostalgia and enjoy this mighty main meal soup with the family for a Saturday lunch. Little else is needed except a healthy appetite.

Serves 4

low fat cooking spray
1 large onion, sliced finely
2 large carrots, cut into 1 cm (½ inch) slices
2 celery sticks, sliced
250 g (9 oz) swede, cut into chunks
65 g (2½ oz) pearl barley
500 g (1 lb 2 oz) chicken thighs, skinless but on the bone
1.5 litres (2¾ pints) hot chicken or vegetable stock
350 g (12 oz) mushrooms, sliced thickly
1 teaspoon dried sage (or 1 tablespoon finely chopped fresh)
2 tablespoons cornflour
2 teaspoons Worcestershire sauce
2 tablespoons freshly chopped parsley
salt and freshly ground black pepper

5½ *POINTS* values per serving
23 *POINTS* values per recipe

270 calories per serving

Takes **30 minutes** to prepare, **40 minutes** to cook

✻ recommended

1 Spray a large lidded casserole dish or saucepan with low fat cooking spray. Stir fry the onion, carrots, celery and swede for 5 minutes until slightly softened. Add the pearl barley and the chicken pieces. Continue to stir fry for 3–4 minutes, or until the chicken is lightly coloured.

2 Add the stock and bring to the boil, then lower the heat, cover and simmer gently for 35–40 minutes. (During this time the barley will swell and soften, absorbing some of the stock.)

3 Use tongs to remove the cooked chicken to a chopping board. Add the mushrooms and sage to the saucepan, and continue to simmer, uncovered, for 10 minutes. Meanwhile, remove the chicken flesh from the bones and shred roughly. Return the meat to the saucepan. Season to taste.

4 Blend the cornflour to a paste with the Worcestershire sauce and a drop of cold water. Stir into the broth and continue to heat through until the broth thickens slightly. Check the seasoning.

5 Ladle into warm bowls, scatter on the parsley and serve immediately.

Tips Choose chicken thighs or legs for the best flavour and succulence.

Dark-gilled open mushrooms will add more flavour and depth to this broth than button mushrooms, so look out for them.

Avocado, Tomato and Cucumber Salad

This refreshing salad is delicious and it's a great way of making the smooth, delicate flavour of avocado go a long way.

Serves 4

12 Cos or Romaine lettuce leaves
225 g (8 oz) tomatoes, chopped
1 small avocado, peeled and diced
½ cucumber, diced
2 tablespoons olive oil
½ teaspoon finely grated lemon zest
2 tablespoons lemon juice
1 small garlic clove, crushed
2 teaspoons Dijon mustard
salt and freshly ground black pepper
2–3 tablespoons freshly chopped coriander, mint or basil (or all three), to garnish

2½ **POINTS** values per serving
10 **POINTS** values per recipe

C 140 calories per serving

Takes 10 minutes

V

* not recommended

1 Arrange three lettuce leaves on each of four serving plates.

2 Mix together the tomatoes, avocado and cucumber and pile into the lettuce leaves.

3 Make the dressing by mixing together the olive oil, lemon zest and juice, garlic and mustard. Season to taste.

4 Spoon the dressing over the salads and serve at once, scattered with the herbs.

Tips Use a mixture of tomatoes for a variety of flavours – Sungold, cherry and vine tomatoes taste delicious together.

Eat wisely Salad leaves are a great way to add interest and bulk to your meals, without adding any **POINTS** values. Try to vary the salad leaves you buy, until you find one you like.

Sweet Potato and Sausage Salad

Roasted sweet potatoes are delicious eaten hot or cold and make a great salad ingredient, especially when combined with sausage and a creamy mustard dressing.

Serves 4

4 sweet potatoes
low fat cooking spray
8 thin low fat sausages
4 shallots, chopped finely
a small bunch of fresh chives, chopped
salt and freshly ground black pepper

For the dressing
4 tablespoons half fat crème fraîche
1 tablespoon Dijon mustard

4½ *POINTS* values per serving
18½ *POINTS* values per recipe

190 calories per serving

Takes **15 minutes** to prepare + cooling,
30 minutes to cook

* not recommended

1 Preheat the oven to Gas Mark 7/220°C/fan oven 200°C. Scrub the potatoes and cut into wedges. Place in a roasting tin, spray with the low fat cooking spray, season then roast for 30 minutes until tender.

2 Meanwhile, preheat the grill and grill the sausages for about 5 minutes on each side until browned and cooked through. Leave to cool, then chop into pieces.

3 Heat a non stick frying pan and spray with the cooking spray, then stir fry the shallots for 5 minutes until softened, adding a little water if necessary to stop them from sticking.

4 Place the sweet potato, sausages, shallots and chives in a bowl. In a separate bowl stir together the dressing ingredients, then spoon over the potatoes. Toss the salad together and serve.

Variation Use ordinary potatoes instead of sweet potatoes.
The *POINTS* values per serving will be 4.

Cook's note As an alternative to roasting, put the sweet potatoes into a large pan of boiling water or stock for 10–12 minutes.

Lemony Chicken Salad

This is a very quick and refreshing lunch salad – or you could divide it into six portions for a starter, each with a **POINTS** value of 2½ per serving.

Serves 4

150 g (5½ oz) fusilli bucati (short spirals)
500 g (1 lb 2 oz) cooked chicken breasts,
  skin removed and torn into strips
10 cm (4 inch) piece of cucumber, diced
4 spring onions, chopped
16 cherry tomatoes, halved
8 tablespoons fat free dressing
2 tablespoons tarragon, freshly chopped
zest of a lemon, finely grated
salt and freshly ground black pepper

4 POINTS values per serving
15½ POINTS values per recipe

334 calories per serving

Takes **20 minutes** + **30 minutes** chilling
(optional)

✻ not recommended

1 Bring a large pan of water to the boil, add the pasta and cook for 10–12 minutes or according to the packet instructions. Drain and rinse in plenty of cold water.

2 Toss in the rest of the ingredients and mix to combine. Season to taste.

Tip Chill the salad for 30 minutes before serving to allow the flavours to develop.

Variation Serve the salad with torn Cos lettuce leaves for extra crunch.

Eat wisely Always try to make your own lunches – it doesn't have to be laborious. Shop bought lunches (whether it's a sandwich or a salad) can be deceptively high in fat. Making your own not only means that you will be able to control what you are eating more effectively, but you'll also save money.

Turkey Ciabatta Grills

Turkey rashers make a tasty topping for these grilled open sandwiches.

Serves 4

1 ciabatta loaf with sun-dried tomatoes
  or olives
2 tablespoons sun-dried tomato paste
150 g (5½ oz) grilled red and yellow
  pepper strips
8 medium turkey rashers, uncooked
salt and freshly ground black pepper
a few basil leaves

4½ *POINTS* values per serving
18 *POINTS* values per recipe

225 **calories** per serving

Takes **10 minutes**

* not recommended

1 Preheat the grill to high.

2 Slice the loaf in half lengthways and spread with the tomato paste.

3 Top both pieces of ciabatta with the pepper strips, then the uncooked turkey rashers. Grill for 1½ minutes, then turn the rashers over and grill for another 1½ minutes, until the rashers are cooked.

4 Slice each piece of bread in half, season to taste and scatter with a few basil leaves. Serve immediately.

Tip Look for grilled pepper strips in jars, preserved in vinegar, then rinse and drain them. Alternatively, you can buy canned red peppers (sometimes called pimientos) which simply need to be drained and sliced.

Pitta Pockets with Roasted Vegetables

Serves 4

250 g (9 oz) courgettes, cut into chunks
2 red onions, cut into wedges
1 aubergine, cubed
2 small green peppers, de-seeded and diced
2 tablespoons balsamic vinegar
low fat cooking spray
200 g (7 oz) cherry tomatoes, halved
150 g (5½ oz) low fat soft cheese with garlic
  and herbs, cubed
4 medium pitta breads
salt and freshly ground black pepper

4 POINTS values per serving
16½ POINTS values per recipe

C **264 calories** per serving

Takes **15 minutes** to prepare,
30 minutes to cook

V

* not recommended

1 Preheat the oven to Gas Mark 5/190°C/fan oven 170°C. Line a roasting tin with non stick baking parchment.

2 In a large mixing bowl, mix together the courgettes, onions, aubergine and green peppers with the balsamic vinegar and seasoning. Spray with a little low fat cooking spray.

3 Arrange the vegetables in the roasting tin and cook for 25 minutes, turning them halfway through. Remove from the oven and mix in the tomatoes and cheese. Return to the oven for 5 minutes.

4 Warm the pitta breads in the oven for the last 5 minutes of the roasting time.

5 Split the warm pittas lengthways. Pile the cooked mixture into the breads and serve.

Tip Balsamic vinegar can be quite expensive – choose the best you can afford as a little goes a long way. Its sweet, sticky flavour is quite different to ordinary vinegar.

Individual Roasted Vegetable Pizzas

These pizzas are great to eat at lunchtime with friends as they are heaped with delicious roasted vegetables and are very substantial.

Serves 4

1 butternut squash, peeled and cut into chunks
1 red onion, peeled and cut into wedges
8 baby carrots, tops trimmed
1 red pepper, de-seeded and diced
3 sprigs of rosemary
low fat cooking spray
1 x 144 g packet pizza base mix
4 teaspoons olive oil
1 garlic clove, peeled and crushed
12 cherry tomatoes
salt and freshly ground black pepper

3 POINTS values per serving
11½ POINTS values per recipe

270 calories per serving

Takes **25 minutes** to prepare + **10 minutes** proving, **50 minutes** to cook

V

✳ not recommended

1 Preheat the oven to Gas Mark 6/ 200°C/fan oven 180°C. Place the squash, onion, carrots and pepper, with two sprigs of rosemary, in a large roasting tin, spray with low fat cooking spray and toss so that they are evenly coated. Roast for 40 minutes, turning occasionally, until the vegetables are tender and beginning to char. Remove from the oven and discard the sticks from the rosemary, leaving any loose leaves. Increase the oven temperature to Gas Mark 7/220°C/fan oven 200°C.

2 Meanwhile, make up the pizza base according to the packet instructions. Divide the dough into four and knead to make 12 cm (4½ inch) rounds. Place on a baking sheet sprayed with low fat cooking spray and leave to rise for 10 minutes.

3 Remove the leaves from the remaining rosemary sprig and chop finely. Mix with the olive oil and garlic and season.

4 Top the pizza bases with the roasted vegetables and cherry tomatoes and drizzle over the oil. Bake for 12–15 minutes until golden. Serve hot or cold.

Tip Cook the vegetables up to 24 hours in advance, then cover and chill until required.

Chick Pea Falafel with Cucumber and Mint Dressing

Serves 4

low fat cooking spray
1 small onion, finely chopped
1 garlic clove, crushed
1 teaspoon ground coriander
1 teaspoon ground cumin
½ teaspoon chilli flakes
1 x 425 g (15 oz) can chick peas, drained
1 egg
25 g (1 oz) wholemeal breadcrumbs
3 tablespoons freshly chopped coriander
salt and freshly ground black pepper
some shredded lettuce, to serve

For the dressing

150 ml (5 fl oz) low fat natural yogurt
2 tablespoons mint jelly
175 g (6 oz) cucumber, diced finely

---

3 POINTS values per serving
13 POINTS values per recipe

C   **162 calories** per serving

Takes **25 minutes** to prepare,
20 minutes to cook

V

*   recommended (falafel only)

1 Heat a non stick frying pan and spray with low fat cooking spray. Gently cook the onion and garlic until softened but not browned. Stir in the coriander, cumin and chilli flakes. Cook for 1 minute and then remove from the heat. Place in a food processor with the chick peas, egg, breadcrumbs, seasoning and coriander.

2 Blend until evenly combined and then, using clean hands, shape the mixture into about 20 small balls.

3 Preheat the oven to Gas Mark 5/190°C/fan oven 170°C. Arrange the falafel on a non stick baking sheet and cook for 20 minutes.

4 To make the dressing, mix together the yogurt and mint jelly. Stir in the cucumber. Season to taste.

5 Serve the cooked falafel on a bed of shredded lettuce, drizzled with the mint and cucumber dressing.

Cooking basics To slice an onion finely: if you don't have a food processor, but need to slice onions finely, peel off the skin but don't cut off the root at the bottom. Slice the onion in half then slice it from the top, but don't cut through the root as this holds the onion together. Now slice horizontally across the vertical cuts. Finally, chop off the roots and discard. You should have very finely sliced onion.

Thai Fish Cakes

Crab cakes are a Thai speciality – and no wonder, as they taste so good. Serve them with a zero **POINTS** value vegetable stir fry or salad.

Serves 4

2 teaspoons sesame oil
75 g (2¾ oz) long grain rice
3 shallots or 1 small onion, chopped
1 large garlic clove, crushed
2 tablespoons freshly chopped coriander
1 x 170 g can of crabmeat, drained
1 tablespoon Thai fish sauce or light
   soy sauce
200 ml (7 fl oz) reduced fat coconut milk
2 eggs, beaten
2 teaspoons Thai red curry paste
salt and freshly ground black pepper
spring onions, red chillies and sprigs of
   fresh coriander, to garnish

4½ **POINTS** values per serving
17 **POINTS** values per recipe

225 calories per serving

Takes **20 minutes** to prepare,
25–30 minutes to cook

* recommended

1 Preheat the oven to Gas Mark 4/180°C/fan oven 160°C. Grease four 200 ml (7 fl oz) ramekins with ½ teaspoon of the oil.

2 Cook the rice in plenty of boiling water for about 12 minutes, until just tender. Rinse with cold water and drain well.

3 Heat the remaining oil in a small frying pan and sauté the shallots or onion and garlic for about 5 minutes, until softened and golden brown.

4 In a large bowl, mix together the rice, shallots or onion, garlic, coriander, crabmeat, fish sauce or soy sauce, coconut milk, eggs and curry paste. Season.

5 Divide the mixture between the ramekins. Bake for 25–30 minutes, until set.

6 Leave to cool slightly, then turn them out and serve, garnished with finely sliced spring onions, red chilli and fresh coriander.

Eat wisely It can be tempting to buy ready made, shop bought varieties of fish cakes or fish fingers as a quick and easy family meal. However, making your own version, like in the recipe above, not only tastes better but is a much healthier alternative for all the family – and the extra effort is minimal.

Greek Spinach and Filo Pie

This Greek dish, also called Spanakopita, is popular all over the Mediterranean.

Serves 4

500 g (1 lb 2 oz) spinach, washed, tough
  stems removed and chopped
low fat cooking spray
1 onion, chopped finely
a bunch of spring onions, chopped finely,
  including the green tops
a small bunch of flat leaf parsley,
  chopped finely
a small bunch of dill, chopped finely
¼ teaspoon grated nutmeg
100 g (3½ oz) low fat soft cheese
100 g (3½ oz) plain cottage cheese
8 sheets of filo pastry
salt and freshly ground black pepper

2½ **POINTS** values per serving
9½ **POINTS** values per recipe

C   235 calories per serving

Takes **30 minutes** to prepare,
45 minutes to cook

V

✱   not recommended

1 Preheat the oven to Gas Mark 3/160°C/fan oven 140°C. Place the wet spinach in a saucepan with the lid on and cook for 4 minutes until completely wilted. Transfer to a colander and press down with a wooden spoon to extract the moisture. Then put it in a large bowl.

2 Spray a frying pan with the low fat cooking spray and sauté the onion for 5 minutes, stirring occasionally. Add the spring onions and cook for a further 2 minutes. Add them to the spinach with the herbs, nutmeg, seasoning and cheeses. Beat everything together with a wooden spoon.

3 Spray a metal 23 cm (9 inch) square baking tin or ovenproof dish with the cooking spray. Cover the bottom of the tray with five sheets of pastry, one on top of the other, spraying each with a little cooking spray as you lay them down, and folding them up and over the sides of the dish.

4 Spread the spinach mixture over the filo, then cover with the remaining three sheets, spraying between each layer as well as on top.

5 Score through the top sheets of pastry with a knife to make diamond shaped portions, which will make cutting them up easier later (cut diagonally to the right and then to the left). Sprinkle with a little water to prevent the pastry curling and brush lightly to spread the water evenly.

6 Bake for 45 minutes until golden and crispy. Allow to stand for a few minutes before cutting into portions and serving.

Tip To prevent the filo pastry drying out while you are working, cover any unused sheets with a damp tea towel.

Soufflé Baked Potatoes

Simple baked potatoes take on an exciting new character with a light cheese and onion filling. Serve these with a crisp zero *POINTS* value salad.

Serves 4

4 large (approx 300 g/10½ oz each) baking
  potatoes
low fat cooking spray
a large bunch of spring onions, sliced finely
8 tablespoons skimmed milk
100 g (3½ oz) cherry tomatoes, quartered
2 egg whites
100 g (3½ oz) half fat Cheddar cheese, grated
salt and freshly ground black pepper

 5 *POINTS* values per serving
22½ *POINTS* values per recipe

C **332 calories** per serving

⊘ Takes **15 minute**s to prepare,
1 hour 15 minutes to cook

V

✳ not recommended

1 Preheat the oven to Gas Mark 5/190°C/fan oven 170°C. Prick the potatoes all over with a fork and bake for 1 hour, or until soft.

2 Meanwhile spray a frying pan with the low fat cooking spray and stir fry the spring onions until just tender and golden.

3 Cut the potatoes in half and scoop out the flesh into a large bowl. Add the milk and mash together until you have a smooth blend.

4 Stir in the fried spring onions and the tomatoes and season. Whisk the egg whites until stiff and fluffy and then fold carefully into the potato mixture with the grated cheese.

5 Place the potato skins on a baking tray and refill them with the potato mixture, piling up high. Bake for 10–15 minutes, until golden and hot. Serve immediately.

Tip If you don't have the time to bake your potato in the oven, then just pop the potato into the microwave on a high heat for 7–8 minutes until soft in the middle.

Macaroni Cheese Gratins

The whole family will love these cheesy little pots. And since they're made in individual dishes, everyone gets their own.

Serves 4

150 g (5½ oz) quick cook macaroni
2 tablespoons cornflour
300 ml (10 fl oz) skimmed milk
a pinch of ground nutmeg
75 g (2¾oz) half fat Cheddar cheese, grated
low fat cooking spray
1 tablespoon Worcestershire sauce
175 g (6 oz) carrots, peeled and grated
1 red onion, sliced thinly
1 courgette, wiped and grated
1 tablespoon dried breadcrumbs
1 tablespoon grated Parmesan cheese
salt and freshly ground black pepper

To serve
iceberg lettuce, shredded
cucumber, peeled and chopped

4½ POINTS values per serving
17 POINTS values per recipe

282 calories per serving

Takes 20 minutes to prepare,
35 minutes to cook

V

* recommended

1 Bring a pan of water to the boil and cook the macaroni as directed on the packet. Drain well.

2 Meanwhile, mix the cornflour with a little of the milk to form a thin paste. Heat the remaining milk until boiling and pour over the cornflour paste. Mix well and return to the heat. Cook, stirring for 2–3 minutes until you have a smooth thickened sauce.

3 Stir the nutmeg and grated cheese into the sauce. Then add the drained macaroni and stir well.

4 Preheat the oven to Gas Mark 5/190°C/fan oven 170°C.

5 Spray a lidded non stick frying pan with low fat cooking spray and add the Worcestershire sauce, grated carrot, onion and courgette. Cover and cook for 2–3 minutes to just soften. Season to taste and then divide between four individual ramekins. Top with macaroni cheese.

6 Mix together the breadcrumbs and Parmesan and sprinkle over the top. Bake for 15 minutes, then serve hot with a salad garnish.

Cooking basics How to cook pasta: place the pasta in a large saucepan. Add plenty of boiling water to allow the pasta to swell up and move (otherwise the pasta will become sticky). Cook until the pasta is just tender or al dente.

Tofu Kebabs with Peanut Sauce

Treat yourself to an exotic Thai style main meal, served with a luxurious peanut sauce that is unbelievably low in **POINTS** values.

Serves 4

2 x 200 g packets of tofu, cut into bite size squares
4 tablespoons light soy sauce
2 teaspoons sesame oil
2 large garlic cloves, crushed
1 red pepper, de-seeded, cut into bite size squares
1 yellow pepper, de-seeded, cut into bite size squares
2 Little Gem lettuce, shredded, to serve

For the sauce

2 spring onions, chopped finely
½ teaspoon chilli powder
1 teaspoon caster sugar
4 teaspoons white wine vinegar
2 tablespoons crunchy peanut butter

 3½ **POINTS** values per serving
13 **POINTS** values per recipe

C 319 **calories** per serving

⏱ Takes **30 minutes** to prepare

V

✳ not recommended

1 Mix the tofu together with 2 tablespoons of the soy sauce, the sesame oil and garlic. Leave it to marinate for 5 minutes.

2 Thread the tofu and pepper pieces alternately on to wooden satay sticks.

3 In a small saucepan, place the sauce ingredients together with the remaining soy sauce and heat for 2–3 minutes until just hot and blended together.

4 Preheat the grill to a high heat. Grill the tofu kebabs for about 5–6 minutes, turning them once, until they are crispy. Serve the kebabs on the shredded lettuce with the sauce spooned over.

> **Cooking basics** How to make the most of tofu: tofu doesn't have much flavour, but it absorbs the flavours it is cooked with like a sponge. Always allow enough time to marinate it properly and use liquid marinades, such as soy sauce, that will soak into the tofu.

Welsh Rarebit

It's hard to find a more classic combination than simple toast with cheese. This recipe is recognised all over the world as one of the great simple dishes. It's quick, easy to make and inexpensive, so it's a favourite with families.

Serves 4

100 g (3½ oz) low fat soft cheese with garlic and herbs
40 g (1½ oz) Caerphilly, grated finely
a few drops of mushroom ketchup or soy sauce
½ teaspoon wholegrain mustard
4 medium slices of white or wholemeal bread
freshly ground black pepper
4 tomatoes, sliced, to serve
salad leaves, to garnish (optional)

ℂ 3 *POINTS* values per serving
11 *POINTS* values per recipe

C 141 calories per serving

⊘ Takes 20 minutes

V

✳ not recommended

1 Preheat the grill to a medium heat.

2 In a small bowl, mix together the soft cheese and Caerphilly, mushroom ketchup or soy sauce and mustard. Season with a little freshly ground black pepper.

3 Lightly toast the bread on both sides. Spread the cheese mixture on top, and then grill until golden and bubbling.

4 Serve at once with the tomatoes, garnished with salad leaves, if using.

Variations Use plain low fat soft cheese if you prefer and, if you want to spice up your Welsh rarebit, add a few drops of chilli sauce instead of the mushroom ketchup or soy sauce, for the same *POINTS* values.

For a more substantial meal, top with well-drained lightly cooked spinach and a poached egg. The *POINTS* values per serving will be 4.

Eat wisely For many of us cheese is our downfall – if it's in the fridge we'll eat it. A great solution is to grate your cheese into weighed out portions (e.g. 40 g/1½ oz) and then store these individual portions in bags in the freezer. When you want to use it, simply take out a bag and let it thaw for about an hour before using.

Turkey and Spinach Samosas

These are great to take on a picnic or in your lunchbox to the office. If you love really spicy food then just increase the chilli powder to your liking. Try serving these samosas with a crisp green salad for no additional **POINTS** values.

Makes 15

low fat cooking spray
1 small onion, diced finely
1 garlic clove, crushed
280 g (9¾ oz) turkey mince
1 teaspoon ground cumin
1 teaspoon ground coriander
1 teaspoon chilli powder
½ teaspoon ground ginger
175 g (6 oz) frozen chopped spinach,
   defrosted and drained
15 sheets of 2½ x 43½ cm filo pastry
salt and freshly ground black pepper

1 **POINTS** value per serving
17½ **POINTS** values per recipe

75 calories per serving

Takes **35 minutes** to prepare,
15 minutes to cook

recommended for up to 1 month

1 Preheat the oven to Gas Mark 6/ 200°C/fan oven 180°C.

2 Spray a medium saucepan with low fat cooking spray. Add the onion, garlic and turkey mince and cook for 5–6 minutes, stirring occasionally to brown the meat.

3 Add the spices and stir well before adding the spinach and seasoning. Mix together and heat to a gentle simmer. Simmer for 15 minutes.

4 Leave the mixture to cool slightly. Lay the filo pastry on the work surface. Lay one sheet on a chopping board large enough for the whole sheet. Spray the pastry with the cooking spray and then lay another sheet on top. Repeat this until you have three sheets of filo on top of each other.

5 Cut the stack of filo sheets lengthways into three.

6 Place a heaped tablespoon of the turkey and spinach mixture at the bottom of each strip of pastry. To fold into a samosa shape, lift one of the corners at the bottom of the pastry strip (nearest the filling) and bring it diagonally over the filling to the other side. This will give you a triangle shape. Pick up the point of the triangle and fold the filled pastry over diagonally. Keep folding over and over until you reach the top of the pastry strip and have a triangular samosa.

7 Repeat the process with the remaining pastry and turkey mixture to make 15 samosas.

8 Place the samosas on a baking sheet and spray them with the cooking spray.

9 Bake the samosas in the oven for 15 minutes until golden.

Spring Rolls

These tasty, crunchy vegetable and prawn rolls have all the flavour of those served in Chinese restaurants, but they are only a fraction of the **POINTS** values since they are baked and not deep fried.

Serves 4

low fat cooking spray
100 g (3½ oz) carrots, sliced into thin strips
100 g (3½ oz) white cabbage, shredded
1 small red pepper, de-seeded and
 sliced thinly
100 g (3½ oz) fresh prawns, peeled
100 g (3½ oz) fresh beansprouts
2 tablespoons dark soy sauce, plus extra
 for dipping
¼ teaspoon Chinese 5 Spice powder
8 x 14 g sheets of filo pastry

1½ **POINTS** values per serving
6½ **POINTS** values per recipe

136 calories per serving

Takes **20 minutes** to prepare,
15 minutes to cook

✳ not recommended

1 To make the filling, spray a large frying pan with low fat cooking spray. Add the carrots, cabbage, red pepper, prawns, beansprouts, soy sauce and 5 Spice powder. Stir fry for 2 minutes. Remove the pan from the heat and allow the mixture to cool a little.

2 Preheat the oven to Gas Mark 5/190°C/fan oven 170°C. Line a baking sheet with non stick baking parchment.

3 Spray a sheet of filo pastry with a little cooking spray. Spoon some of the filling on to one end of the pastry sheet. Roll the pastry up, tucking in the edges to enclose the filling so that you end up with a sausage shape. Repeat this process with the remaining pastry sheets until you have eight spring rolls.

4 Place the spring rolls on the baking sheet and bake for 10 minutes until they are golden and crispy. Serve them hot with extra soy sauce for dipping, allowing two spring rolls per person.

Store cupboard ideas Soy sauce is an essential condiment, particularly if you like Oriental food. You can use it to colour and flavour marinades, dips and sauces. Light soy sauce has a delicate, salty flavour that goes well with white meats and seafood. Use dark soy sauce, which is thicker, richer but less salty, with meats or in stews.

Veggie Burgers

Delicious burgers, stuffed full of vegetables and served with a tasty Californian salsa.

Serves 4

400 g (14 oz) potatoes, peeled and quartered
500 g (1 lb 2 oz) mixed zero *POINTS* value
 vegetables
low fat cooking spray
2 leeks, chopped roughly
1 garlic clove, chopped
2 tablespoons soy sauce
1 tablespoon tomato purée
1 egg, beaten
a small bunch of parsley, freshly chopped
salt and freshly ground black pepper

For the salsa

100 g (3½ oz) cherry tomatoes, quartered
½ cucumber, diced finely
2 tablespoons tomato juice
1 small red onion, chopped finely
1 teaspoon horseradish sauce

 2 *POINTS* values per serving
9 *POINTS* values per recipe

C **208 calories** per serving

Takes **30 minutes**

V

✱ not recommended

1 Cook the potatoes in boiling water for 15 minutes until tender, then drain. Meanwhile, cook the mixed vegetables in boiling water for 5 minutes and drain.

2 Heat a non stick frying pan and spray with the low fat cooking spray. Fry the leeks and garlic for 10 minutes until softened and golden.

3 Mash the potatoes, then add the vegetables and other ingredients, including the cooked leeks and garlic. Season and mix well.

4 Shape the mixture into eight burgers. Heat a large non stick frying pan and spray with the cooking spray. Fry the burgers for 4–5 minutes on each side.

5 Meanwhile, mix all the salsa ingredients together in a bowl. Serve two burgers each with the salsa.

Store cupboard ideas Herbs are always good to have to hand. You can add so much flavour, without any fat, by simply adding a sprinkling of herbs to your dishes. Experiment until you find your favourite varieties, and then always try to keep some stashed. You can buy dried or fresh herbs from all the supermarkets – and if you are really ambitious you can even try growing your own.

Simply Quiche

This scrumptious version of Quiche Lorraine has far fewer *POINTS* values than the original. Serve hot or cold with a zero *POINTS* value mixed salad or vegetables.

Serves 4

4 medium slices bread
4 teaspoons low fat spread
2 rashers lean back bacon
2 eggs, beaten
220 g (7½ oz) low fat cottage cheese
2 tablespoons finely chopped onion
salt and freshly ground black pepper

4 *POINTS* values per serving
16½ *POINTS* values per recipe

203 calories per serving

Takes **10 minutes** to prepare,
15–20 minutes to cook

✳ recommended

1 Preheat the oven to Gas Mark 6/200°C/fan oven 180°C.

2 Flatten the slices of bread with a rolling pin until thin, then spread with the low fat spread. Use the slices (spread side up) to line a flan case, about 23 cm (9 inches) in diameter.

3 Grill the bacon rashers until crisp, then snip into small pieces. Mix with the eggs, cottage cheese and onion. Season.

4 Pour the mixture into the bread-lined flan case. Bake in the centre of the oven until set, about 20 minutes.

Tip For individual portions, cook the quiche in Yorkshire pudding tins or tartlet tins.

Variation Use 4–5 chopped spring onions instead of the onion.

Vegetarian variation If you are vegetarian, omit the bacon and use some chopped vegetables instead – courgettes and peppers would be ideal – for 3½ *POINTS* values per serving.

Minced Meat Kebabs

On the streets of Morocco, Tunisia and Algeria, these fragrant kebabs are served in warmed pitta breads with a sprinkling of salt and cumin.

Serves 4

400 g (14 oz) lean minced lamb
a small bunch of parsley, chopped
a small bunch of coriander, chopped
1 onion, chopped finely
½ teaspoon ground allspice
¼ teaspoon cayenne pepper
1 teaspoon ground cumin
1 teaspoon paprika
low fat cooking spray
salt and freshly ground black pepper
4 medium pitta breads, to serve

4½ *POINTS* values per serving
17½ *POINTS* values per recipe

210 **calories** per serving

Takes **30 minutes** + **1 hour** chilling

not recommended

1 Mix all the ingredients except the low fat cooking spray to a smooth paste in a bowl.

2 With moistened hands, take generous tablespoons of the paste and mould it into 10-cm (4-inch) long finger shapes around four wooden or metal skewers. Refrigerate for 1 hour.

3 Preheat the grill and cover a grill pan with foil. Spray with the cooking spray, then put the skewers on it and grill for 4 minutes on each side. To serve, slice each pitta bread open and slide the kebabs off the skewers into the pittas.

Tips If the mince falls off the skewers in step 2, put it in the fridge for 30 minutes and try again.

If using wooden skewers, soak them in hot water for 10 minutes before using so that they will not burn under the grill.

These are delicious with 1 tablespoon tzatziki dip and 1 tablespoon reduced fat hummous; just remember to add the extra 1½ *POINTS* values per serving.

Fish Goujons with Tartare Sauce

Serve these crisp coated fish pieces as finger food, with the creamy tartare sauce as a dip.

Serves 6

100 g (3½ oz) plaice, skinned and cut in
  thick strips
50 g (1¾ oz) plain flour, seasoned with
  ½ teaspoon chilli powder
2 large egg whites, beaten
300 g (10½ oz) fresh breadcrumbs
lemon wedges, to serve

For the tartare sauce

100 g (3½ oz) low fat soft cheese
200 ml (7 fl oz) very low fat natural
  fromage frais
2 tablespoons capers, rinsed and squeezed
  to remove excess vinegar
4 small gherkins, chopped finely
2 spring onions, chopped finely
a small bunch of fresh dill or fennel, chopped
salt and freshly ground black pepper

3 *POINTS* values per serving
17½ *POINTS* values per recipe

201 **calories** per serving

Takes **35 minutes**

✳ not recommended

1 Preheat the grill to a medium heat. Dip some of the fish strips first in the chilli flour, then in the egg whites and finally in breadcrumbs. Spread out on a grill pan lined with foil.

2 Grill the goujons until golden and crisp and cooked through, turning over once or twice to brown all over. Repeat with the remaining fish strips.

3 Meanwhile, make the tartare sauce by beating together the soft cheese and fromage frais and then stirring in all the other ingredients with some seasoning. Tip into a serving bowl and serve with the goujons, with the lemon wedges to squeeze over.

BBQ Chicken Drumsticks

A perfect family lunch for a summer weekend.

Makes 12 drumsticks

12 medium skinless chicken drumsticks

For the marinade
2 garlic cloves, crushed
2.5 cm (1 inch) piece of fresh root ginger,
  peeled and grated
finely grated zest of 2 oranges
juice of an orange
1 small red chilli, de-seeded and
  chopped finely
2 tablespoons clear honey
2 tablespoons soy sauce
2 tablespoons tomato purée
½ tablespoon sesame oil

1½ *POINTS* values per serving
17½ *POINTS* values per recipe

88 calories per serving

Takes **10 minutes** to prepare + **4 hours** marinating, **15–25 minutes** to cook

✳ recommended

1 Mix all the marinade ingredients together in a small bowl. Put the drumsticks in a non-metallic dish, add the marinade and turn the drumsticks to make sure they are well coated. Leave to marinate in the refrigerator for at least 4 hours, but preferably overnight.

2 Preheat the grill to a medium heat or ensure your barbecue is ready. Cook the drumsticks for 15–25 minutes, or until they are thoroughly cooked and golden brown. (A grill will take longer than a hot barbecue.)

Cooking basics To cut and de-seed chillies: carefully slice the chilli in half vertically. Use a teaspoon to scrape out the seeds and throw them away. Cut away the white membrane. Slice the chillies very finely and add to the dish. Wash your hands thoroughly.

Tandoori Turkey Bites

Kids love these spicy little turkey bites.

Serves 4

2 tablespoons tandoori paste
2 teaspoons lemon juice
6 tablespoons low fat natural yogurt
2 tablespoons chopped fresh mint
450 g (1 lb) turkey steaks, cut into
 2.5 cm (1 inch) chunks

3 POINTS values per serving
12 POINTS values per recipe

151 calories per serving

Takes **10 minutes** to prepare + **1–4 hours** marinating, **15 minutes** to cook

recommended

1 Mix together the tandoori paste, lemon juice, yogurt and mint in a non-metallic bowl.

2 Add the turkey, stir well, then cover and refrigerate for 1–4 hours. The longer the meat is left to marinate, the more intense the flavour will be.

3 Thread the cubes of turkey on to eight skewers. Cook under a medium-high preheated grill or barbecue for about 15 minutes, turning occasionally, and serve.

Tip Wooden kebab sticks should be soaked in hot water for about 10 minutes before use, to prevent them from burning when grilling.

Variation Balti curry paste can be used instead of tandoori paste, for the same **POINTS** values.

Roast Chicken with Rosemary and Lemon Potatoes

A Sunday lunch regular – this roast never fails to please. The potatoes need to be parboiled for around 15–20 minutes before you start.

Serves 4

1 x 1.5 kg (3 lb 5 oz) whole chicken
2 lemons, 1 cut into wedges the other cut in half
a small bunch of rosemary, leaves removed from the stalks and chopped
400 g (14 oz) potatoes, cut into wedges and parboiled
low fat cooking spray
300 ml (10 fl oz) chicken stock
salt and freshly ground black pepper

3½ *POINTS* values per serving
13 *POINTS* values per recipe

345 calories per serving

Takes **15 minutes** to prepare,
1 hour 15 minutes to cook

✱ not recommended

1 Preheat the oven to Gas Mark 6/200°C/fan oven 180°C. Place the chicken in a large roasting tray and season all over. Squeeze the juice from the halved lemon over the skin of the chicken and then place the squeezed lemon 'shells' inside the cavity of the chicken with half the rosemary.

2 Place the lemon wedges and potatoes around the bird. Spray with the low fat cooking spray, season and sprinkle with the remaining rosemary. Roast for 1¼ hours, basting occasionally with any juices in the tray, turning and basting the potatoes too.

3 To test if the chicken is cooked, stick a skewer or knife into the meatiest portion of one of the thighs. The juices should run clear.

4 When cooked, remove the chicken from the roasting tray to a carving board, cover with foil and keep warm while you make the gravy.

5 To make the gravy, remove the potatoes and lemon wedges to serving bowls and keep warm. Drain off any excess fat and place the roasting tray on the hob. Heat until the juices boil and then add the stock.

6 Scrape up any juices stuck to the tin with a wooden spoon or spatula and boil rapidly for a few minutes until reduced a little. Strain the gravy into a jug and serve with three skinless slices of chicken per person, garnished with the roasted lemon wedges and the roast potatoes.

Beef Fillet with Horseradish Crust

What's more traditional than roast beef and Yorkshire pudding? A real family treat.

Serves 8

1 kg (2 lb 4 oz) lean fillet of beef, in one
   piece or boned and rolled sirloin
150 g (5½ oz) mushrooms, chopped
a bunch of rosemary, chopped finely
4 tablespoons horseradish sauce
200 g (7 oz) fresh breadcrumbs
low fat cooking spray
salt and freshly ground black pepper

For the Yorkshire puddings
100 g (3½ oz) plain flour
1 egg
300 ml (10 fl oz) skimmed milk

For the gravy
2 teaspoons plain flour
300 ml (10 fl oz) vegetable stock

5½ *POINTS* values per serving
43½ *POINTS* values per recipe

C   370 calories per serving

Takes 20 minutes to prepare, 1 hour to
cook + 10 minutes resting time

✳   not recommended

1 Preheat the oven to Gas Mark 7/220°C/fan oven 200°C. With a sharp knife make a slit along the side of the fillet then open it up to make a pocket. Mix the mushrooms with half the rosemary and seasoning and stuff inside the fillet.

2 Season the outside of the fillet and then spread all over with the horseradish sauce. Spread the breadcrumbs on a large plate and roll the fillet in them until they are stuck all over.

3 Spray a roasting tin with the low fat cooking spray and place the fillet in it. Cover with a piece of foil.

4 Roast the beef on a lower shelf for 30 minutes. Take off the foil and brown for a further 15 minutes for a medium-cooked fillet. For a well-done fillet, brown for 30 minutes. Remove the beef from the oven and place on a carving board, loosely covered with the foil again, to keep warm and allow to rest for 10 minutes before carving.

5 Meanwhile, for the Yorkshire puddings, prepare the batter by mixing the flour with a pinch of salt in a large bowl. Make a well in the middle and crack in the egg, add the milk and 100 ml (3½ fl oz) water. Gradually stir in the flour until you have a smooth batter.

6 Put a baking tin or patty tin with 12 individual moulds in the oven, on the top shelf, for 5 minutes, until very hot. Using an oven glove remove the tin from the oven, spray with low fat cooking spray and quickly pour in the batter. Return it to the top shelf and bake for 40 minutes, until the puddings are risen and golden. Do not open the oven door while they are cooking.

7 To make the gravy, pour off any fat in the roasting tin and then set it on the hob. Sprinkle over the flour and mix it in with the juices using a wooden spatula. Add the remaining rosemary and stock and boil rapidly, scraping up any stuck on juices with the spatula. Season and pour into a serving jug.

Simply Suppers

There's nothing better at the end of the day than quick and easy family suppers that are satisfying, healthy and full of good ingredients. Try pasta dishes, such as Spinach and Ricotta Cannelloni; one-pot meals, such as Sausage and Bean Hotpot; recipes from around the world, like Mediterranean Turkey Rolls; and modern twists on family favourites, such as Mini Toad in the Hole.

Make the most of your evenings by having supper together as a family

Prawn and Chilli Tagliatelle

A hot and spicy recipe with big juicy prawns. Temper the heat with a cooling yogurt sauce.

Serves 4

225 g (8 oz) tagliatelle
low fat cooking spray
1 onion, chopped
1 garlic clove, crushed
1 x 400 g can chopped tomatoes
1 tablespoon hot chilli sauce
20 tiger prawns, shelled, defrosted if frozen,
   with tail tip left on (see tip)
1 tablespoon coriander, freshly chopped
salt and freshly ground black pepper

For the dip
150 g pot 0% fat Greek yogurt
1 tablespoon mint, freshly chopped
zest of ½ lemon, grated finely

3½ *POINTS* values per serving
14 *POINTS* values per recipe

C 275 calories per serving

Takes **20 minutes**

✳ not recommended

1 Bring a large pan of water to the boil, add the pasta and cook for 10–12 minutes or according to packet instructions.

2 Meanwhile, for the dip, mix the yogurt, mint and lemon zest together and set aside.

3 Spray a saucepan with low fat cooking spray and heat over a medium heat until sizzling. Add the onion and cook for 5 minutes until softened, then add the garlic and cook for a further 2 minutes.

4 Stir in the tomatoes and chilli sauce, reduce the heat and simmer for 5 minutes until thickened. Stir in the prawns and cook for 2 minutes until hot.

5 Drain the pasta, pour over the prawn sauce and toss to mix. Season and stir in the coriander. Serve with the yoghurt sauce as a dip for the prawns.

Tips If you prefer a creamy sauce, simply combine the yogurt mixture with the tomato sauce.

If you leave the tails on the prawns, they are easier to pick up and dip into the yogurt.

Variation Adjust the amount of chilli sauce to your liking.

Mushroom and Leek Macaroni

Cream and wine go wonderfully well together and this recipe makes the most of half fat crème fraîche to give a really creamy, tasty sauce.

Serves 4

225 g (8 oz) quick cook macaroni
low fat cooking spray
2 leeks, trimmed, washed and sliced
250 g (9 oz) mixed mushrooms (e.g. button, chestnut, oyster), sliced
2 garlic cloves, crushed
125 ml (4 fl oz) dry white wine
1 tablespoon mushroom ketchup or soy sauce
4 tablespoons half fat crème fraîche
3 tablespoons freshly chopped parsley, plus extra for garnish
salt and freshly ground black pepper

4½ POINTS values per serving
18 POINTS values per recipe

C **300 calories** per serving

Takes **20 minutes**

V

✳ not recommended

1 Bring a large pan of water to the boil, add the macaroni and cook for 6–7 minutes or according to the packet instructions. Drain and rinse with boiling water.

2 Meanwhile, spray a frying pan with low fat cooking spray and when it is hot, add the leeks and mushrooms and stir fry over a medium heat for 5 minutes until softened. Add the garlic and continue cooking for 2 minutes until the mushroom juices have evaporated.

3 Add the wine and mushroom ketchup or soy sauce and simmer over a medium heat to reduce the liquid by half. Turn down the heat and stir in the crème fraîche and parsley. Add the pasta and heat for 2 minutes until piping hot. Season and serve garnished with extra parsley.

Tip Make this a store cupboard supper by using dried mushrooms instead of fresh.

Variation Tarragon has a lovely subtle aniseed-like flavour; try substituting it for the parsley.

Penne with Meatballs

A classic recipe with a twist. In this version, turkey mince replaces beef mince, which reduces the *POINTS* values without reducing the delicious flavours.

Serves 4

For the meatballs
low fat cooking spray
1 onion, chopped finely
1 garlic clove, crushed
300 g (10½ oz) turkey mince
1 teaspoon dried mixed herbs
200 g (7 oz) penne
salt and freshly ground black pepper

For the sauce
1 garlic clove, crushed
250 g (9 oz) passata
2 tablespoons shredded basil leaves, plus
   extra for garnish

4 *POINTS* values per serving
16½ *POINTS* values per recipe

300 calories per serving

Takes 40 minutes to prepare and cook
+ 10 minutes chilling

recommended (meatballs only)

1 Spray a large frying pan with low fat cooking spray and heat over a medium heat until hot. Add the onion and cook, stirring, for 5 minutes until beginning to brown. Add the garlic and cook for a further 2 minutes. Remove from the heat and let it cool slightly.

2 Place the turkey mince in a large bowl with the cooked onion and garlic mixture, herbs and seasoning, then mix it all together – you might find it easiest to mix with your hands.

3 Make 20 walnut sized balls, rolling them in your hands until smooth. Cover and chill for 10 minutes to help them bind together.

4 Bring a large pan of water to the boil, add the penne and cook for 10–12 minutes or according to the packet instructions. Drain and rinse with boiling water.

5 Meanwhile, respray the frying pan with cooking spray and cook the meatballs over a medium heat, turning frequently for 8 minutes until golden all over. For the sauce, add the garlic and the shredded basil to the pan with the meatballs and cook over a low heat for 2 minutes, then add the passata. Slowly bring to the boil, reduce the heat and simmer for 2–3 minutes until piping hot.

6 Divide the pasta between four bowls and serve the meatballs on top with the sauce drizzled over and garnished with the basil leaves.

Tips Wet your hands when rolling the meatballs as it makes the meatballs less sticky.

You can make the meatballs and cook them in advance, then simply heat them through in the sauce when you are ready to eat.

Spinach and Ricotta Cannelloni

The whole family will love this quick, filling and tasty dish.

Serves 4

4 sheets of fresh lasagne, measuring
  14½ x 20 cm (5¾ x 8 inches) and
  weighing 188 g (7 oz)
300 g (10½ oz) frozen spinach, defrosted
  and drained
220 g (7½ oz) ricotta cheese
600 g (1 lb 5 oz) passata with herbs
salt and freshly ground black pepper
a handful of fresh basil leaves, torn,
  to garnish

5½ **POINTS** values per serving
21 **POINTS** values per recipe

C 229 calories per serving

Takes **30 minutes**

V

✳ recommended

1 Preheat the oven to Gas Mark 6/200°C/fan oven 180°C. Halve each lasagne sheet to create eight rectangles approximately 7 x 10 cm (3 x 4 inches). Bring a large pan of water to the boil, add the pasta and cook according to the packet instructions. Drain and keep warm.

2 Mix together the spinach and ricotta. Season to taste. Place 2 tablespoons of the spinach mixture in a line in the centre of each rectangle and roll up. Repeat with the other sheets using all the mixture. Place the tubes in an ovenproof dish.

3 Pour the passata over the cannelloni. Bake for 15 minutes until bubbling. Serve garnished with the fresh basil leaves.

Eat wisely When you go to the effort of making a delicious family meal, such as this cannelloni, make it into more of an occasion. Turn off the TV and use the time to chat over the day. You'll find that you enjoy the food more too.

Creamy Chicken Bake

Pop this in the oven to cook while you enjoy time with the family.

Serves 4

low fat cooking spray
300 g (10½ oz) skinless chicken breast, diced
2 small courgettes, sliced
175 g (6 oz) fusilli
600 g (1 lb 5 oz) passata with herbs
200 g tub low fat soft cheese with garlic
  and herbs

4½ *POINTS* values per serving
18½ *POINTS* values per recipe

C 340 calories per serving

Takes **10 minutes** to prepare,
45 minutes to cook

✱ not recommended

1 Preheat the oven to Gas Mark 5/190°C/fan oven 170°C. Heat a frying pan until hot and then spray with low fat cooking spray. Add the chicken pieces and courgettes and stir fry for 3–5 minutes until browned all over.

2 Meanwhile, cook the pasta for 2 minutes only. Drain.

3 Add the passata and 100 ml (3½ fl oz) water to the chicken and courgettes in the pan and stir in. Bring to the boil.

4 Remove from the heat and add the pasta and soft cheese to the chicken. Pour into a baking dish, cover with foil and bake for 45 minutes until the chicken and pasta are cooked. Serve immediately on warmed plates.

Vegetable Risotto

An easy dish that you can put on and leave to cook while you get on with other things. Guaranteed to fill everyone up and you can vary the vegetables according to your family's taste or what is seasonally available.

Serves 4

low fat cooking spray
2 large onions, chopped finely
4 garlic cloves, crushed
2 courgettes, diced finely
2 red peppers, de-seeded and diced finely
450 g (1 lb) mushrooms, sliced
250 g (9 oz) long grain rice
500 ml (18 fl oz) passata
600 ml (20 fl oz) vegetable stock
salt and freshly ground black pepper

3 *POINTS* values per serving
12½ *POINTS* values per recipe

325 calories per serving

Takes 20 minutes to prepare,
30 minutes to cook

V

✳ recommended

1 Spray a large lidded saucepan with the low fat cooking spray and then stir fry the onions and garlic until softened, adding a little water if necessary to prevent them from sticking.

2 Add the other vegetables and stir fry for a few minutes, until golden. Add all the remaining ingredients, stir together and bring to the boil.

3 When boiling, turn down to a low simmer and put the lid on. Leave to cook for 30 minutes or until the rice has absorbed all the water and is tender. Serve immediately on warmed plates.

Cooking basics Make your own vegetable stock: reserve all the trimmings and peel from vegetables and boil them in a pan with 1.2 litres (2 pints) of water, a handful of peppercorns, half an onion, a bay leaf and some herbs. Cook for 1 hour then remove from the heat and strain. The stock will keep in the fridge for a few days or can be frozen.

Sesame Chicken

This is great as a light and fast supper.

Serves 4

**2 skinless, boneless chicken breasts, each
weighing approximately 150 g/5½ oz, cut in
half lengthways**
4 garlic cloves, sliced finely
**2.5 cm (1 inch) piece of fresh root ginger,
grated finely**
4 tablespoons soy sauce
zest and juice of 2 limes
2 teaspoons sesame oil

For the spinach salad
225 g (8 oz) baby spinach leaves
a small bunch of mint, chopped roughly
**a bunch of spring onions, sliced finely
lengthways**

1 Lay the chicken breasts between two pieces of baking parchment, clingfilm or foil and pound with a rolling pin until they become thin escalopes.

2 Place the garlic, ginger, soy sauce, lime zest and juice and sesame oil in a large bowl and add the chicken breasts. Toss the chicken in the marinade and then set aside for at least 5 minutes but preferably 30 minutes.

3 Meanwhile divide the spinach, mint and spring onions between four serving plates or bowls.

4 Remove the chicken from the marinade and grill for 4–5 minutes on each side, or until cooked through and golden. Slice the chicken and place on top of the spinach salad.

5 Heat the leftover marinade in a small pan until boiling, then drizzle over the chicken and salad before serving.

1½ *POINTS* values per serving
7 *POINTS* values per recipe

145 **calories** per serving

Takes **15 minutes** + marinating

not recommended

Cooking basics How to prepare ginger: using a sharp knife, cut the length of ginger you need. Carefully slice off the skin. Holding the ginger at one end, slice it very thinly. Alternatively, use a cheese grater to grate the ginger into fine slices.

Sausage and Bean Hotpot

A one-pot recipe, this just needs some zero *POINTS* value green vegetables to accompany it.

Serves 4

low fat cooking spray
8 thick, low fat sausages
2 onions, sliced
2 garlic cloves, crushed
1 teaspoon dried mixed herbs
1 x 400 g can chopped tomatoes
300 ml (10 fl oz) vegetable stock
2 x 410 g cans cannellini beans, drained and rinsed
salt and freshly ground black pepper

1 Heat the low fat cooking spray in a lidded non stick frying pan and fry the sausages and onions for 5 minutes over a medium heat until browned.

2 Add the garlic and herbs and cook for 30 seconds, then stir in the remaining ingredients. Bring to a simmer, cover and cook for 10 minutes.

3 Remove the lid and cook for a final 5 minutes to thicken the sauce slightly.

4 *POINTS* values per serving
16½ *POINTS* values per recipe

C **267 calories** per serving

⏲ Takes **10 minutes** to prepare, **15 minutes** to cook

✳ recommended

Vegetarian variation For a vegetarian version, simply substitute eight thick vegetarian sausages for the pork sausages, for the same *POINTS* values per serving.

Family Fish Pie

An easy fish pie that's great for a midweek supper. Serve with your favourite zero *POINTS* value vegetables, such as broccoli and carrots.

Serves 6

450 g (1 lb) floury potatoes, peeled and cut
 in chunks
450 g (1 lb) pumpkin or butternut squash,
 peeled, de-seeded and cut in chunks
600 ml (20 fl oz) skimmed milk
2 bay leaves
500 g (1 lb 2 oz) cod fillets
low fat cooking spray
1 large onion, sliced
2 garlic cloves, crushed
4 celery sticks or a small fennel bulb,
 chopped finely
150 g (5½ oz) mushrooms, sliced
100 g (3½ oz) frozen sweetcorn or peas
2 tablespoons cornflour
a small bunch of fresh parsley
1 heaped teaspoon French mustard
100 g (3½ oz) half fat mature Cheddar
 cheese, grated
salt and freshly ground black pepper

> 4 *POINTS* values per serving
> 23 *POINTS* values per recipe

C 277 calories per serving

⊘ Takes **35 minutes** to prepare,
 20 minutes to cook

✳ not recommended

1 Boil the potatoes and pumpkin or butternut squash in a saucepan. Cook for 20 minutes, or until tender. Strain but reserve the cooking liquid. Mash the two together and season.

2 Meanwhile, in a large non stick frying pan, heat the milk with the bay leaves and fish fillets until it comes to the boil and then simmer for 1 minute, or until the fish is almost cooked through. Remove the fish to a plate and then strain the milk into a small saucepan and reserve.

3 Rinse the frying pan and spray with the low fat cooking spray. Fry the onion and garlic for 5 minutes, until softened, adding 1–2 tablespoons of the reserved potato cooking liquid if necessary to prevent them from sticking.

4 Add the celery or fennel and a few more tablespoons of the potato cooking liquid and cook for a further 5 minutes. Add the mushrooms and cook on a high heat for 3 minutes, until the mushrooms start to give out their juices. Remove from the heat. This mixture needs to be dry, so drain off any juices.

5 Break up the fish, removing any skin and bones, and fold into the vegetables with the sweetcorn or peas. Transfer the whole mixture to a large baking dish.

6 Preheat the oven to Gas Mark 6/200°C/fan oven 180°C. Take a couple of tablespoons of the reserved milk and mix with the cornflour. Stir this paste back into the rest of the milk and bring to the boil, stirring, until it thickens; then add the parsley, mustard and seasoning.

7 Pour the parsley sauce over the fish mixture and fold gently together. Top with the potato and pumpkin mash. Scatter over the grated cheese and bake for 20 minutes, until the cheese is golden and bubbling.

Shepherd's Pie

Serve with plenty of zero *POINTS* value vegetables: broccoli, cauliflower or cabbage would be ideal.

Serves 4

900 g (2 lb) potatoes, peeled and quartered
350 g (12 oz) lean, minced lamb
1 large onion, chopped finely
1 large leek, chopped finely
1 carrot, chopped
225 g (8 oz) swede or turnip, peeled and
  chopped
450 ml (16 fl oz) lamb or vegetable stock
2 tablespoons cornflour, blended with
  3 or 4 tablespoons cold water
6 tablespoons skimmed milk
salt and freshly ground black pepper

7 *POINTS* values per serving
27½ *POINTS* values per recipe

C **390 calories** per serving

Takes **30 minutes** to prepare,
50 minutes to cook

✱ recommended

1 Cook the potatoes in boiling water for about 20 minutes, until tender.

2 Meanwhile, heat a large, lidded, non stick saucepan and add the lamb mince, a handful at a time, cooking over a high heat to seal and brown it.

3 Add the onion to the mince with the leek, carrot and swede or turnip and cook for about 3 minutes, stirring often. Pour in the stock, bring to the boil. Cover and simmer for about 20 minutes.

4 Preheat the oven to Gas Mark 5/190°C/fan oven 170°C.

5 Stir the blended cornflour into the lamb mixture. Cook until thickened for about 2 minutes. Remove from the heat.

6 Drain the potatoes and mash them. Add the milk and seasoning and beat vigorously with a wooden spoon until the potatoes are light and fluffy. Alternatively, use a hand-held electric beater to whisk the potatoes for a few moments.

7 Transfer the meat mixture to a 1.2 litre (2-pint) ovenproof dish and top with the mashed potato. Bake for 25–30 minutes until thoroughly heated and browned.

Variation Before baking in the oven, sprinkle the surface of the mash with finely sliced leek and 25 g (1 oz) of grated mature Cheddar for 7½ *POINTS* values per serving.

Vegetarian variation For a vegetarian version, use Quorn mince instead of lamb and be sure to use vegetable stock. The *POINTS* values per serving will be reduced to 4½.

Vegetable Chilli

Bring the flavours of Mexico to your table with this easy-to-make tasty vegetarian chilli.

Serves 4

low fat cooking spray
1 large onion, chopped
2 garlic cloves, crushed
3 celery sticks, chopped finely
1 large carrot, chopped finely
1 courgette, chopped
1 x 350 g pack of Quorn mince
2–3 teaspoons medium chilli powder
1 x 400 g can chopped tomatoes
2 tablespoons tomato purée
1 x 215 g can red kidney beans, rinsed
  and drained
1 x 198 g can sweetcorn with peppers
1 vegetable stock cube, dissolved in 300 ml
  (10 fl oz) boiling water
175 g (6 oz) long grain rice
salt and freshly ground black pepper

5 *POINTS* values per serving
19½ *POINTS* values per recipe

375 **calories** per serving

Takes **15 minutes** to prepare,
30 minutes to cook

V

* recommended

1 Heat a large, lidded saucepan and spray with low fat cooking spray. Add the onion, garlic, celery, carrot and courgette. Stir fry for 2–3 minutes.

2 Add the Quorn mince, chilli powder, tomatoes, tomato purée, red kidney beans, sweetcorn with peppers and stock to the pan. Stir well and bring to the boil. Cover, reduce the heat and simmer for about 30 minutes, stirring from time to time.

3 Around 15 minutes before you're ready to serve, put the rice on to cook in plenty of boiling water. Cook for about 12 minutes until tender, or according to the packet instructions. Drain well and rinse with boiling water.

4 Check the flavour of the chilli, and season according to taste. Divide the cooked rice between four warmed serving plates and pile the cooked chilli on top. Serve at once.

Tips Cook spicy food according to your taste, adding extra chilli powder if you like things spicy, or use it sparingly if you prefer a milder flavour.

Cans of sweetcorn with peppers are available in supermarkets. Although not as quick, you could also use 150 g (5½ oz) sweetcorn and 50 g (1¾ oz) chopped peppers. The *POINTS* values per serving will be 4½.

Szechuan Beef Stir Fry

A tasty stir fry with the most tender beef.

Serves 4

250 g (9 oz) lean beef braising steak, cut into thin strips
1 teaspoon bicarbonate of soda

For the sauce
1 teaspoon cornflour
2 tablespoons tomato purée
1 tablespoon rice or wine vinegar
1 teaspoon chilli powder
1 teaspoon caster sugar
2 teaspoons soy sauce

For the stir fry
2 teaspoons peanut oil
2 garlic cloves, sliced into slivers
2.5 cm (1 inch) piece of fresh root ginger, peeled and sliced into fine matchsticks
a bunch of spring onions, sliced finely
200 g (7 oz) mushrooms, preferably oyster, sliced finely
125 g can water chestnuts, drained

---

2 **POINTS** values per serving
9 **POINTS** values per recipe

160 **calories** per serving

Takes **35 minutes** to prepare + **4 hours** marinating

✳ recommended

1 Put the beef in a bowl with the bicarbonate of soda and just enough water to cover. Leave to marinate in the refrigerator for about 4 hours.

2 In a bowl, mix the cornflour into a paste with 2 tablespoons of water and then mix in all the other sauce ingredients.

3 When ready to cook, drain the beef and pat dry on kitchen paper. Heat the oil in a large frying pan or wok until just smoking then add the beef and toss around the pan for 2 minutes. Add the garlic and ginger and stir fry for another minute.

4 Add all the other ingredients, toss and stir fry over a high heat for 2 minutes. Give the sauce ingredients a stir and pour over. Bring to the boil, stir and serve.

Store cupboard ideas Stir fries are fantastic, flavoursome and a very quick dish to make. Most supermarkets sell ready prepared fresh zero **POINTS** value stir fried vegetables quite cheaply, so that you can just throw the whole packet into the pan for a quick and tasty meal – rather than chopping and preparing your own.

Maple and Mustard Chicken Tray-bake

Great for a mid-week roast, this also cuts down on washing up as it's all cooked together in one tray.

1 Preheat the oven to Gas Mark 6/200°C/fan oven 180°C.

2 Parboil the potatoes in boiling water for 10 minutes. Drain and mix with the onions, courgettes, olive oil and seasoning in a large roasting tin. Place in the oven to cook for 15 minutes.

3 Stir the vegetables around and add the seasoned chicken breasts to the roasting tin. Roast for a further 10 minutes.

4 Mix the maple syrup with the mustard and lemon juice. Stir the vegetables around again, adding the tomatoes, and drizzle the maple mustard glaze all over the chicken and vegetables.

5 Roast for a final 15 minutes.

Store cupboard ideas Onions are an essential store cupboard ingredient and you should always try to keep a stock of them in your kitchen. They are a wonderful base to almost any dish – adding flavour and texture. Experiment to find your favourite – white onions, red onions, shallots, spring onions. Try roasting, sweating, frying – add to casseroles and stir fries or use them in a delicious roast dish like in the recipe above.

Garlic Roast Pork with Mash

Creamy, garlicky mash topped with garlic pork chops.

Serves 4

450 g (1 lb) pork loin
2 garlic bulbs, unpeeled
4 garlic cloves, chopped
600 g (1 lb 5 oz) potatoes, peeled and chopped
125 ml (4 fl oz) skimmed milk
200 g (7 oz) broccoli, cut into florets and
  steamed or boiled, to serve
salt and freshly ground black pepper

6½ **POINTS** values per serving
25½ **POINTS** values per recipe

366 calories per serving

Takes **20 minutes** to prepare,
50 minutes to cook

✳ not recommended

1 Preheat the oven to Gas Mark 7/220°C/fan oven 200°C.

2 Make slits between the pork flesh and the bones and place the meat in a baking dish with the garlic bulbs.

3 Stuff the chopped garlic into the slits in the meat and rub the joint with seasoning. Roast for 25 minutes until golden.

4 Remove the garlic bulbs, set aside and reduce the oven temperature to Gas Mark 4/180°C/fan oven 160°C. Cook the pork for another 25–35 minutes.

5 Meanwhile, cook the potatoes in a pan of boiling water until tender. Drain and add the skimmed milk. Squeeze out the cooked garlic from the bulbs, add to the pototoes and mash together until creamy.

6 Serve the pork, sliced into thick pieces on a bed of garlicky mash with steamed or boiled broccoli.

Store cupboard ideas Garlic is indispensable in cooking – so always keep some bulbs in the fridge. Choose fresh, plump looking garlic with a white skin and a fat neck, as these will have a more delicate flavour. Stick to the specified amount in recipes until you know your taste well – too much garlic will quickly overpower the other flavours in the dish.

Braised Lamb Chops

This makes a traditional and satisfying midweek dinner with a minimum of hassle.

Serves 4

2 tablespoons plain flour
4 lamb leg chops trimmed of all fat,
   weighing approximately 130 g (4½ oz) each
low fat cooking spray
1 large onion, sliced
a small bunch of fresh thyme or marjoram
150 ml (5 fl oz) stock
450 g (1 lb) sweet potatoes, peeled and
   sliced thickly
100 g (3½ oz) mushrooms, sliced
4 beef tomatoes, sliced thickly
salt and freshly ground black pepper

5 **POINTS** values per serving
20 **POINTS** values per recipe

355 **calories** per serving

Takes **30 minutes** to prepare,
1 hour to cook

recommended

1 Put the flour on a plate, season, then roll the chops in it. Heat a large, lidded frying pan and spray with the low fat cooking spray. Brown the lamb for a few minutes on each side then remove from the pan to a plate and set aside.

2 Spray the pan with the cooking spray again and fry the onion for 4 minutes until softened. Add the herbs and the stock, scraping up any juices stuck to the bottom of the pan.

3 Arrange a layer of the sweet potato slices on the bottom of the pan and then top with the lamb. Cover and cook gently for 45 minutes.

4 Add the mushrooms and then a layer of tomato slices. Season and cook for another 15 minutes then serve.

Variation Use ordinary potatoes rather than sweet ones for a more traditional dish. The **POINTS** values per serving will be the same.

Store cupboard ideas Stock is an indispensable ingredient when eating the Weight Watchers way. You should always keep a good supply — either buy stock cubes from the supermarket or make your own. You'll find that stock is often used as a base for soups, casseroles or curries.

One Pot Goulash

This is a great midweek dish as you can assemble it in advance up to the point where you put the casserole in the oven, and then just cook it when you need it. Dill isn't a traditional Hungarian accompaniment, but it is delicious with the tender, slow cooked beef.

Serves 4

2 teaspoons caraway seeds
600 g (1 lb 5 oz) new potatoes
low fat cooking spray
500 g (1 lb 2 oz) lean braising steak, cubed
2 large onions, chopped
2 garlic cloves, crushed
2 red peppers, de-seeded and cut into
 chunks
1 teaspoon hot smoked paprika (see Tip)
2 x 400 g (14 oz) cans chopped tomatoes
2 beef stock cubes, dissolved in 200 ml
 (7 fl oz) boiling water
2 tablespoons freshly chopped dill (optional)
4 tablespoons low fat natural yogurt,
 to serve
salt and freshly ground black pepper

5½ *POINTS* values per serving
21 *POINTS* values per recipe

395 **calories** per serving

Takes **15 minutes** to prepare,
1¾ hours to cook

✱ recommended

1 Preheat the oven to Gas Mark 4/180°C/fan oven 160°C. Using a pestle and mortar or a heavy rolling pin, crush the caraway seeds to release their aroma. Wash the potatoes and cut any large ones in two – leave the rest whole. Put the seeds and potatoes to one side.

2 Spray a large lidded hob and ovenproof casserole dish with the low fat cooking spray and fry the beef for a few minutes until sealed and browned on all sides. You may need to do this in batches. Remove the beef from the pan and set aside.

3 If necessary, spray the pan again and then add the onions, garlic and peppers. Fry for 2–3 minutes to soften them. Return the beef to the pan and stir in the paprika, crushed caraway seeds, tomatoes, stock and potatoes.

4 Put the lid on the casserole dish, place it in the oven and cook for 1¾ hours or until the meat is tender. Stir occasionally.

5 Before serving, check the seasoning and stir in the chopped dill, if using. Divide between four large, warmed bowls and top each with a tablespoon of yogurt.

Tip As the name suggests, hot smoked paprika is hotter than its milder counterpart and it adds a lovely smoky depth to this dish. If you're using standard sweet paprika, use 4 teaspoons.

Sweet, Sticky, Peppered Pork

A quick and easy recipe with vibrant flavours. Serve with 150 g (5½ oz) cooked brown rice per person and a zero **POINTS** value salad, adding 3 **POINTS** values per serving.

Serves 4

2 tablespoons reduced-sugar marmalade
4 pork escalopes, weighing approximately
 150 g (5½ oz) each
2 tablespoons peppercorns, crushed
low fat cooking spray

For the sauce
2 tablespoons balsamic vinegar
150 ml (5 fl oz) orange juice
1 tablespoon whole grain mustard
1 teaspoon cornflour, made into a paste with
 a tablespoon of water

3½ **POINTS** values per serving
14 **POINTS** values per recipe

260 calories per serving

Takes **25 minutes**

not recommended

1 Gently heat the marmalade in a pan with 2 tablespoons of water, then brush over the pork escalopes. Place the crushed peppercorns on a plate and press the escalopes down on to them so that the meat becomes covered with pepper.

2 Heat a non stick pan and spray with the low fat cooking spray. Fry the escalopes in two batches for 2–3 minutes on each side until cooked through, then set aside and keep them warm while you make the sauce.

3 With the pan still on the heat, pour in the vinegar and scrape up all the left over juices and bits left from the pork with a wooden spatula or spoon. Pour in the orange juice and stir in the mustard and cornflour and bring to the boil. Boil for 1 minute, stirring, until the sauce has thickened.

4 Serve the pork with the sauce poured over.

Tip For a more attractive dish, buy mixed peppercorns, which include red, white and black ones.

Baked Cheesy Leeks

This dish is best made with the young tender leeks at the start of the season, which is early autumn.

Serves 4

low fat cooking spray
12 small leeks, trimmed and slit in half from
  top to bottom, then washed
4 eggs
200 g (7 oz) low fat soft cheese
200 g (7 oz) low fat plain yogurt
50 g (1¾ oz) rye crispbreads
salt and freshly ground black pepper
a few sprigs of fresh thyme, chopped, to
  serve (optional)

3½ **POINTS** values per serving
14½ **POINTS** values per recipe

C 254 calories per serving

Takes **20 minutes** to prepare,
40 minutes to cook

V

✳ not recommended

1 Preheat the oven to Gas Mark 4/180°C/fan oven 160°C. Spray a shallow ovenproof dish with the low fat cooking spray. Blanch the leeks by putting them in a saucepan of boiling water for 6–8 minutes, until just tender. Drain and arrange them in the ovenproof casserole dish.

2 Meanwhile beat the eggs with the soft cheese and yogurt and some seasoning. Break up the crispbreads by putting them in a plastic bag and pounding them with a rolling pin or do this in a food processor. Pour the cheese sauce over the leeks and scatter with the crispbread crumbs.

3 Bake for 35–40 minutes, until the top is crisp and brown and the sauce is bubbling. Serve scattered with the thyme, if using.

Store cupboard ideas Rye crispbreads are a good low **POINTS** value alternative to bread. Use them in your lunch box with sandwich ingredients, or experiment with more creative ideas – such as replacing breadcrumb bases with the crisp base. Each rye crispbread has a **POINTS** value of ½.

Mediterranean Turkey Rolls

Basil complements turkey so well in these tasty rolls that the whole family will enjoy.

Serves 4

2 aubergines
2 red peppers
100 g (3½ oz) ricotta cheese
a large bunch of basil, freshly chopped,
  with a few chopped leaves reserved
8 thin turkey escalopes (about 400 g/14 oz
  in total)
low fat cooking spray
1 garlic clove, crushed
2 tablespoons white wine vinegar
1 x 400 g can chopped tomatoes
1 teaspoon clear honey
salt and freshly ground black pepper

5½ *POINTS* values per serving
22 *POINTS* values per recipe

205 **calories** per serving

Takes **45 minutes** + cooling

* not recommended

1 Preheat the oven to Gas Mark 6/ 200°C/fan oven 180°C. Place the whole aubergines and red peppers on a baking tray and bake for 20 minutes. Then leave to cool.

2 Meanwhile, put the ricotta in a bowl with half the chopped fresh basil and season. Season the turkey escalopes and then put them between two sheets of baking parchment, foil or clingfilm. Beat with a rolling pin or meat-tenderising mallet until thin but not broken.

3 When the peppers are cool enough to handle, peel and de-seed them and then chop them finely. Mix with the ricotta and remaining basil. Put spoonfuls of this along one end of the turkey escalopes and then roll them up. Line a baking tray with foil and spray with the cooking spray. Place the rolls on the foil and bake in the oven for 10 minutes until golden and cooked through.

4 In the meantime, slice the aubergines in half lengthwise, scoop out all the flesh and chop well. Spray a frying pan with the cooking spray and sauté the garlic for 2 minutes, then add the white wine vinegar and the aubergine flesh.

5 Cook for 2 minutes, stirring, then add the tomatoes, seasoning, the reserved basil leaves and honey. Cook for 10 minutes. Check the seasoning and then serve poured over the turkey rolls.

Cooking basics How to choose an aubergine: aubergines can vary in colour, so this is not necessarily a good indicator. Look for firm, heavy aubergines that have no brown patches and a cleft at the wider end.

Tuscan Beans

A simple, aromatic garlic and herb bean dish that is great on its own or as an accompaniment to fish or meat; add the extra **POINTS** values as necessary.

Serves 4

low fat cooking spray
4 garlic cloves, crushed
2 x 400 g cans cannellini beans, rinsed and drained, or dried beans (see Cooking basics, below)
2 tablespoons olive oil
3 sage leaves, chopped finely
juice of ½ a lemon
a small bunch of parsley, chopped
salt and freshly ground black pepper

3 **POINTS** values per serving
12 **POINTS** values per recipe

C 170 calories per serving

Takes 15 minutes

V

* not recommended

1 Heat a large saucepan and spray with the low fat cooking spray. Fry the garlic for 2 minutes until just softened, then add the beans, olive oil, sage and seasoning and toss together for a few minutes until heated through.

2 Add the lemon juice and parsley, stir and serve.

Cooking basics How to cook dried beans, such as borlotti, cannellini, flack, flageolet, kidney, butter etc: To serve 4, place 200 g (7 oz) of dried beans in a large bowl, add enough water to cover the beans plus an extra couple of inches. Add a pinch of bicarbonate of soda and leave to soak overnight. Drain and rinse the beans, place in a saucepan, cover with water plus an extra couple of inches. Add half a peeled onion, 2–3 garlic cloves, a handful of mixed herbs (thyme, rosemary, sage, parsley, bay or coriander). Bring to the boil and boil vigorously for 10 minutes. Reduce the heat and simmer for between 50 minutes and 2 hours, topping up the water during cooking time if necessary. Add a teaspoon of salt towards the end of the cooking time (if it is added at the beginning it will cause the beans to remain tough). Cooking time will depend on the type and age of the beans; push the tip of a small knife into a bean to check for tenderness after about 50 minutes. When tender, drain, remove any vegetables and herbs and use the beans as required.

Summer Vegetable Casserole

Serve this bright and tasty stew with a generous portion of green beans or sugar snap peas for no extra *POINTS* values.

Serves 4

low fat cooking spray
2 onions, chopped
2 garlic cloves, crushed
2 small aubergines, cubed
2 large red peppers, de-seeded and diced
450 g (1 lb) potatoes, cubed
4 teaspoons fennel seeds, crushed
2 x 400 g (14 oz) can chopped tomatoes
200 ml (7 fl oz) dry white wine
4 courgettes, sliced
salt and freshly ground black pepper

1½ *POINTS* values per serving
7 *POINTS* values per recipe

246 calories per serving

Takes 45 minutes

V

* not recommended

1 Heat a large, lidded saucepan and spray with the low fat cooking spray. Add the onions and garlic and stir fry for 2–3 minutes, until golden, adding a little water if necessary to prevent them from sticking.

2 Add the remaining ingredients, except the courgettes, and bring to the boil. Cover and simmer for 20 minutes, until the potatoes are cooked through.

3 Remove the lid, add the courgettes and simmer for a further 5 minutes until they are tender and the casserole is thick. Check the seasoning before serving.

Eat wisely One of the most common causes of over eating is because the food is there. And the reason it is there is because it was picked up at the supermarket. Try to write out a shopping list for all the ingredients you require for your week. Then make sure you're not hungry when you go shopping.

Mini Toad in the Hole

A fun way to serve up this family favourite; just add gravy (see tip below) and your favourite zero *POINTS* values vegetables.

Serves 4 (makes 12 puddings)

1 tablespoon sunflower oil
12 thin, low fat sausages
1 large onion, sliced
125 g (4½ oz) plain flour
1 egg
300 ml (10 fl oz) skimmed milk
salt and freshly ground black pepper

4½ *POINTS* values per serving
18½ *POINTS* values per recipe

114 calories per serving

Takes **15 minutes** to prepare,
20 minutes to cook

not recommended

1 Preheat the oven to Gas Mark 7/220°C/fan oven 200°C.

2 Divide the oil between the hollows in a 12 hole muffin tin (¼ teaspoon in each) and heat in the oven for 2 minutes.

3 Twist each of the sausages in half to form two cocktail sized sausages, and snip to separate.

4 Place two sausages and some onion in each hollow and cook in the oven for 8 minutes until lightly browned.

5 Meanwhile, sift the flour into a bowl and season. Make a well in the centre, break in the egg, and gradually whisk in the milk to give a smooth batter. Transfer to a jug.

6 When the sausages and onions are browned, pour in the batter, dividing it equally between the hollows. Return to the oven and cook for 18–20 minutes until the batters are risen, crisp and a rich golden brown. Serve three puddings per person.

Tip To make gravy, use 4 teaspoons gravy granules made up with 250 ml (9 fl oz) boiling water, for an extra ½ *POINTS* value per serving.

Vegetarian variation For a vegetarian version, use eight medium vegetarian sausages, each cut into three chunks. Place two chunks in each hollow of the muffin tin and follow the rest of the method above. The *POINTS* values will be 5 per serving

Sizzled Chicken with Parsley Mash

This dish is ideal for the whole family, including children.

Serves 4

25 g (1 oz) plain flour
2 teaspoons dried sage
450 g (1 lb) skinless boneless chicken
 breasts, cut into chunks
1 tablespoon vegetable oil
2 garlic cloves, sliced finely
1 onion, sliced
2 apples, cored and chopped but unpeeled
1 chicken stock cube dissolved in 150 ml
 (5 fl oz) hot water
150 ml (5 fl oz) unsweetened apple juice
125 g (4½ oz) mushrooms, sliced
700 g (1 lb 9 oz) potatoes, cut into chunks
4 tablespoons skimmed milk
2 tablespoons freshly chopped parsley, plus
 extra to garnish
salt and freshly ground black pepper

5 POINTS values per serving
19½ POINTS values per recipe

400 calories per serving

Takes **30 minutes** to prepare,
25 minutes to cook

recommended

1 Sprinkle the flour and dried sage on to a plate and season. Roll the pieces of chicken in this mixture.

2 Heat the vegetable oil in a large flameproof casserole or lidded saucepan and add the chicken, cooking over a medium heat until browned on all sides. Push to one side, then add the garlic, onion and apples and sauté for about 3 minutes.

3 Add the stock and apple juice, bring up to the boil, then cover and cook over a low heat for 20–25 minutes, adding the mushrooms after 15 minutes.

4 Meanwhile, cook the potatoes until tender. Mash well, adding the milk and parsley. Season to taste and serve with the chicken, garnished with extra chopped parsley.

Tip Check out the herb and spice racks for some excellent seasonings.

Fish 'n' Chips

A low *POINTS* value version of the traditional family favourite.

Serves 4

900 g (2 lb) potatoes
low fat cooking spray
4 x 200 g (7 oz) skinless cod fillets
1 small egg, beaten
100 g (3½ oz) fresh white breadcrumbs
lemon slices, to serve

6 *POINTS* values per serving
24½ *POINTS* values per recipe

437 calories per serving

Takes **10 minutes** to prepare,
25 minutes to cook

not recommended

1 Preheat the oven to Gas Mark 6/200°C/fan oven 180°C. Line two baking sheets with non stick baking parchment.

2 Peel the potatoes and cut into chips. Place in a large container with a tight-fitting lid and spray with low fat cooking spray. Place the lid on the container and shake thoroughly so the potatoes get coated with a thin film of the spray. Arrange on a baking sheet and cook for about 25 minutes.

3 Meanwhile, make sure there are no bones in the fish fillets. Dip the fish into beaten egg and then into the breadcrumbs to coat evenly. Place on to the other baking sheet and spray with the cooking spray, turning it over so that both sides get coated.

4 Bake on the oven shelf below the chips for 20 minutes. Serve hot with the lemon slices and oven chips.

Tip Leave the skins on the potatoes if you wish.

Variation Serve with a tomato salsa. To make it, just de-seed and dice two ripe tomatoes. Mix with 1 teaspoon chopped fresh herbs and 1 teaspoon of balsamic vinegar, for no additional *POINTS* values.

Basque Chicken Casserole

Most of the cooking for this delicious dish is done in the oven without you having to worry about it.

Serves 4

low fat cooking spray
4 x 175 g (6 oz) skinless boneless chicken
  breasts
225 g (8 oz) shallots, peeled but left whole
2 garlic cloves, crushed
1 x 400 g (14 oz) can chopped tomatoes
½ teaspoon paprika
2 red, yellow or orange peppers, de-seeded
  and chopped
2 bay leaves
150 ml (5 fl oz) dry white wine
salt and freshly ground black pepper

To serve

1 tablespoon capers
grated zest of a lemon
a small bunch of fresh basil, chopped
1 small red chilli, de-seeded and chopped
  finely (optional)

3 **POINTS** values per serving
12 **POINTS** values per recipe

265 **calories** per serving

Takes **25 minutes** to prepare,
1 hour to cook

recommended

1 Preheat the oven to Gas Mark 2/150°C/fan oven 130°C. Heat a large non stick frying pan and spray with the low fat cooking spray. Season the chicken breasts, then fry for 5–6 minutes until golden.

2 At the same time, in a large flameproof casserole dish also on the hob, fry the shallots and garlic with the cooking spray for 4 minutes, until starting to brown. Add a little water if necessary to prevent them from sticking. Add the tomatoes, 100 ml (3½ fl oz) of water, the paprika, peppers, bay leaves, white wine and seasoning.

3 Bring to the boil. Add the chicken breasts, incorporating any juices from the base of the pan, and stir well. Cover and cook in the oven for 1 hour.

4 Remove from the oven, check the seasoning and sprinkle with the capers, lemon zest, chopped basil and chilli, if using, to serve.

> **Cooking basics** How to make the most of red peppers: red peppers are not only delicious, but are also great in stir fries, risottos or roasted. They are also excellent stuffed and baked.

Chicken Tikka Masala

Serves 4

2 tablespoons tikka masala curry paste
1 x 150 g tub 0% fat Greek style yogurt
450 g (1 lb) skinless boneless chicken breasts,
  cut into chunks
low fat cooking spray
1 red onion, sliced thinly
1 teaspoon freshly grated root ginger or
  1 teaspoon ready prepared 'fresh' ginger
1 x 400 g can chopped tomatoes
150 ml (5 fl oz) chicken stock
2 tablespoons freshly chopped coriander
100 g (3½ oz) basmati rice
salt and freshly ground black pepper

To garnish

5 cm (2 inch) piece of cucumber, chopped
  finely
a few sprigs of fresh coriander

1 Put the curry paste into a non-metallic bowl and mix in the yogurt, reserving 60 g (2 oz) of it for later. Add the chicken, stir well and then cover and leave to marinate in the fridge for at least 1 hour or overnight.

2 When ready to cook, heat a large non stick saucepan and spray with low fat cooking spray. Add most of the onion, reserving some for garnish. Sauté for 1–2 minutes and then add the ginger and marinated chicken mixture. Cook for 2–3 minutes.

3 Add the tomatoes, stock and chopped coriander to the saucepan. Bring up to the boil, then reduce the heat and simmer, uncovered, over a low heat for 20–25 minutes. Season to taste.

4 When the chicken has simmered for 10 minutes, put the rice on to cook in plenty of boiling water according to the packet instructions.

5 Serve the rice with the cooked chicken, garnished with the reserved yogurt, remaining red onion, cucumber and coriander sprigs.

4 *POINTS* values per serving
16 *POINTS* values per recipe

274 **calories** per serving:

Takes **15 minutes** to prepare + 1 hour marinating, **25 minutes** to cook

recommended

Vegetarian variation Use the same quantity of Quorn pieces instead of the chicken for a vegetarian alternative. The *POINTS* values per serving will remain the same.

Chicken and Spring Onion Burgers

Serves 4

500 g (1 lb 2 oz) chicken or turkey mince
6 spring onions, chopped finely
3 garlic cloves, crushed
2 tablespoons freshly chopped parsley
zest and juice of 1 lime
low fat cooking spray
salt and freshly ground black pepper

To serve

4 medium burger buns
2 tablespoons tomato ketchup
salad leaves, tomato and cucumber

1 Mix together the mince, spring onions, garlic, parsley, lime zest and seasoning. Shape into four patties then heat a non stick frying pan and spray with the low fat cooking spray. Fry the patties for 5–10 minutes on each side until cooked through.

2 Meanwhile, split the buns and toast lightly. Spread each half with ½ tablespoon of tomato ketchup then arrange the salad on the base of each bun and place a burger on top. Squeeze a little lime juice over, replace the top half of the bun and serve.

5 **POINTS** values per serving
19½ **POINTS** values per recipe

270 **calories** per serving

Takes **20 minutes**

not recommended

Tip Serve with 125 g (4½ oz) low fat oven chips per person, for an additional 2½ **POINTS** values per serving.

Easy Pizzas

Everyone loves pizza, and this low *POINTS* values version provides a simple but satisfying meal.

Serves 2

low fat cooking spray
1 small onion, chopped
1 x 200 g can chopped tomatoes with herbs
1 tablespoon tomato purée
1 x 23 cm (9 inch) thin and crispy pizza base
  weighing approx 100 g (3½ oz)
a choice of zero *POINTS* value toppings
  (e.g. mushrooms, pepper strips, cherry
  tomatoes, lightly steamed broccoli
  florets, rocket, baby spinach, thin slices of
  red onion, capers, gherkins)
fresh herbs such as basil, parsley or oregano
  for the topping
salt and freshly ground black pepper

2½ *POINTS* values per serving
5 *POINTS* values per recipe

C 275 calories per serving

⏲ Takes 40 minutes

V

✳ recommended (freeze pizza bases and
  sauce separately)

1 To make the sauce, spray a small non stick saucepan with the low fat cooking spray and fry the onion until soft, adding a little water if necessary to stop it from sticking. Add the tomatoes, tomato purée and seasoning.

2 Bring to the boil and then simmer on a low heat for 10–15 minutes, until thick. Turn off the heat and allow to cool.

3 While the sauce is cooking, preheat the oven to Gas Mark 7/ 220°C/fan oven 200°C. Spoon the tomato sauce on to the pizza base and spread it out evenly to the edges.

4 Decorate the pizzas with the zero *POINTS* values toppings of your choice and then bake for 15–20 minutes, until the edges are golden brown and the vegetables are charred. Scatter with the fresh herbs and serve.

Store cupboard ideas When you have an easy to multiply, freezeable recipe like these pizzas, try to make up two or three batches so you can freeze some for later. Divide into portions and freeze the extra batches you don't need so that you can just pull them out of the freezer and defrost them when you want.

Pancetta Pizza

Pancetta is Italian streaky bacon, usually smoked and often found diced for casseroles, pasta or, as here, pizzas.

Serves 4

low fat cooking spray
1 x 144 g pack pizza base mix
1 x 130 g pack pancetta cubetti
150 g (5½ oz) whole baby portobello or
　closed cap mushrooms, halved
1 red pepper, de-seeded and sliced
2 garlic cloves, peeled and sliced
5 tablespoons passata
2 tablespoons grated half fat Cheddar cheese

5 *POINTS* values per serving
20½ *POINTS* values per recipe

281 **calories** per serving

Takes **25 minutes** to prepare,
20 minutes to cook

✳ not recommended

1 Preheat the oven to Gas Mark 7/220°C/fan oven 200°C. Spray a baking sheet with low fat cooking spray. Mix the dough according to the packet instructions, making one large pizza about 20 cm (8 inches) in diameter.

2 Heat a large frying pan and dry fry the pancetta over a medium heat for 3–4 minutes until browned. Remove from the pan. Spray the pan with the cooking spray and heat until sizzling. Add the mushrooms and pepper and cook over a medium heat for 5 minutes. Add the garlic and cook for a further 2 minutes until the mushroom juices have evaporated. Remove from the heat.

3 Spread the passata over the pizza base, top with the mushroom mixture and cooked pancetta and sprinkle over the cheese. Bake for 15–20 minutes until golden and bubbling.

Tip Use four lean or extra lean back bacon rashers, cut in thin strips if you can't find diced pancetta. The *POINTS* values will be 4 per serving.

Variation Use two 165 g (5¾ oz) chicken breasts, cut in strips, instead of the pancetta. Spray the frying pan with low fat cooking spray and stir fry for 5 minutes until golden and cooked through. The *POINTS* values will be reduced to 3½ per serving.

Meatloaf

A contemporary version of this British classic that's much lower in fat and higher in nutrients and fibre than a traditional recipe. Serve hot with steamed zero *POINTS* value vegetables or cold with a zero *POINTS* value salad. The meatloaf will keep, covered, in the fridge for a few days.

Serves 4

low fat cooking spray
250 g (9 oz) turkey mince
250 g (9 oz) fresh breadcrumbs
1 large onion, grated
2 courgettes, grated
2 carrots, grated
2 tablespoons tomato purée
1 egg, beaten
a small bunch of sage or thyme, chopped,
  reserving a few sprigs or whole leaves for
  garnish
salt and freshly ground black pepper

3½ *POINTS* values per serving
15 *POINTS* values per recipe

365 **calories** per serving

Takes **15 minutes** to prepare,
1 hour to cook

✱ recommended

1 Preheat the oven to Gas Mark 4/180°C/fan oven 160°C. Spray a 1 litre (1¾ pint) loaf tin with the low fat cooking spray and then line with baking parchment.

2 Mix together all the ingredients, except the herbs for the garnish, and pack into the tin. Cover with a piece of foil and bake for 1 hour or until the loaf begins to shrink away from the sides of the tin. Remove the foil for the last 15 minutes to brown the top.

3 Serve in slices, garnished with the reserved herbs.

Store cupboard ideas Tomato purée is a great product, which you should always try to keep in stock. It's made from concentrated tomatoes, adding a great tomato flavour to your dishes.

Savoury Tarte Tatin

The colourful topping of this upside down tart will begin to caramelise as it cooks, giving it a lovely thick glaze.

Serves 4

175 g (6 oz) courgettes, sliced
1 red onion, cut into thin wedges
225 g (8 oz) open cup mushrooms, halved
1 garlic clove, crushed
a sprig of fresh rosemary, chopped
1 tablespoon olive oil
1 teaspoon balsamic vinegar
175 g (6 oz) small tomatoes, halved
2 teaspoons plain white flour, for rolling
175 g (6 oz) puff pastry
salt and freshly ground black pepper

5 *POINTS* values per serving
19½ *POINTS* values per recipe

245 calories per serving

Takes **30 minutes** to prepare,
20 minutes to cook

V

✱ recommended

1 Preheat the oven to Gas Mark 6/200°C/fan oven 180°C.

2 Mix together the courgettes, red onion, mushrooms, garlic, rosemary, olive oil, balsamic vinegar and seasoning. Arrange them on a non stick baking sheet lined with baking parchment and roast for 15 minutes.

3 Remove the vegetables from the oven. Arrange all the vegetables, including the tomatoes, on the base of a 20 cm (8 inch) non stick frying pan or cake tin.

4 Roll out the pastry on a lightly floured surface to make a 23 cm (9 inch) circle. Lay the pastry over the vegetables, tucking in the edges all the way round. Bake the tart in the oven for 20 minutes until the pastry is well risen and golden.

5 Carefully run a round bladed knife around the edge of the pan or tin. Put a large plate over the top and turn the pan or tin upside down, so the tart drops on to the plate. Cut the tart into quarters to serve.

Tip Make sure that if you are using a frying pan for this recipe it has a metal or ovenproof handle, otherwise use a round cake tin.

Variations Use other vegetables, such as de-seeded and diced red or green peppers or cubes of aubergine, in place of any of those used here.

If you like, replace the olive oil with low fat cooking spray and save 1 *POINTS* value per serving. Just spray the vegetables when they are on the baking sheet in step 2.

Quorn Fajitas

A great tasting vegetarian version of this Mexican favourite.

Serves 4

2 tablespoons tomato ketchup
2 tablespoons dark soy sauce
2 garlic cloves, crushed
1 teaspoon chilli flakes
3 x 100 g (3½ oz) Quorn fillets, cut into
   long strips
low fat cooking spray
225 g (8 oz) courgettes, sliced
2 red onions, cut into thin wedges
1 red pepper, de-seeded and sliced
8 flour tortillas
4 tablespoons low fat natural yogurt
2 tablespoons freshly chopped coriander
½ Iceberg lettuce, shredded, to garnish

5½ *POINTS* values per serving
22 *POINTS* values per recipe

400 **calories** per serving

Takes **25 minutes**

V

* not recommended

1 In a bowl, mix the tomato ketchup, soy sauce, garlic and chilli flakes. Add the Quorn and mix well.

2 Preheat the oven to Gas Mark 7/220°C/fan oven 200°C.

3 Spray a griddle pan or non stick frying pan with the low fat cooking spray and heat it until it just starts smoking. Add the Quorn strips, courgettes, onions and pepper to the pan. Cook them for 5–6 minutes over a high heat, until everything is piping hot and beginning to char around the edges.

4 Wrap the tortillas in foil and heat them in the oven for 5 minutes.

5 Divide the filling between the eight tortillas, drizzle over a little yogurt, scatter on the coriander and roll them up tightly. Serve the fajitas with a garnish of shredded Iceberg lettuce, allowing two per serving.

Tip The tortillas can also be warmed on high in the microwave set on high. Depending on the power of your microwave, they will take roughly 30 seconds each – but don't wrap them in foil.

Turkey and Mushroom Potato Topped Pie

Serves 4

low fat cooking spray
1 large onion, chopped
3 rashers lean back bacon
500 g (1 lb 2 oz) turkey breast meat, cut into
  bite size pieces
275 g (9½ oz) mushrooms, sliced thickly
300 ml (10 fl oz) chicken stock
5 or 6 sprigs of fresh thyme
900 g (2 lb) potatoes, peeled and chopped
2 leeks, sliced
100 g (3½ oz) low fat natural fromage frais
3 tablespoons skimmed milk
salt and freshly ground black pepper

5½ *POINTS* values per serving
22½ *POINTS* values per recipe

396 **calories** per serving

Takes **40 minutes** to prepare,
15 minutes to cook

* not recommended

1 Preheat the oven to Gas Mark 6/200°C/fan oven 180°C. Heat a large non stick pan with low fat cooking spray and cook the onion and bacon for 3–4 minutes. Add the turkey and cook for 5–6 minutes before adding the mushrooms, stock, thyme and seasoning. Simmer for 15 minutes.

2 Meanwhile cook the potatoes in a pan of boiling water until tender. Spray a non stick frying pan with the cooking spray and fry the leeks.

3 When the turkey is cooked, stir in the fromage frais and, using a slotted spoon, spoon the mixture into an ovenproof dish. Pour in half of the liquid discarding the rest.

4 Mash the potatoes with the skimmed milk and then using a fork, stir in the leeks. Season well.

5 Top the turkey mixture with the potatoes and leeks and place in the oven for 15 minutes.

Cooking basics To clean mushrooms: in order to retain the full flavour of the mushrooms, clean them by gently wiping them with a clean, damp cloth rather than washing them. Dry them with a paper towel.

Delicious
Desserts

Not everyone has a sweet tooth, but most grown ups – and children – like something
'for afters'. This chapter includes popular puddings and family favourites, including
Roly Pavlova, Strawberry and Hazelnut Strata and Quick Fruit Crumble. Try new
recipes too – everyone is sure to love home made ice creams such as Montezuma
Ice Cream with Marshmallows.

Enjoy these delicious
low fat versions of family favourites

Montezuma Ice Cream with Marshmallows

Montezuma was an Aztec king who was reported to have drunk vast quantities of a rich, dark, spiced, hot chocolate every day.

Serves 6

500 g (1 lb 2 oz) 0% fat Greek yogurt
50 g (1¾ oz) plain chocolate (preferably 70% cocoa solids), melted
a pinch of allspice
a pinch of ground ginger
1 tablespoon honey
2 x 22 g sachets instant, low fat, dark hot chocolate powder, each mixed to a paste with 2 tablespoons of boiling water
100 g (3½ oz) mini marshmallows

4½ **POINTS** values per serving
17 **POINTS** values per recipe

C 175 **calories** per serving

Takes **10 minutes** + freezing

V

✳ recommended

1 Place all the ingredients, except the marshmallows, in a large bowl and blend until smooth and evenly mixed. Fold in the marshmallows and then tip the mixture into a freezer container or ice cream maker and freeze.

2 If not using an ice cream maker, remove the ice cream from the freezer every hour and mash with a fork to break up the ice crystals.

3 Remove the ice cream from the freezer 30 minutes before you want to serve it, to allow it to soften.

Eat wisely If you enjoy your chocolate hit, use high cocoa content chocolate (70% or more) in your cooking. This way you'll still get the same strong chocolate taste, but you use less.

Home Made Vanilla Ice Cream

A delicious, velvety smooth ice cream for an irresistible, low *POINTS* values treat.

Serves 6

600 ml (20 fl oz) skimmed milk
1 vanilla pod, split
2 egg yolks
25 g (1 oz) caster sugar
25 g (1 oz) cornflour
150 ml (5 fl oz) 0% fat Greek style yogurt

1½ *POINTS* values per serving
9 *POINTS* values per recipe

C 115 calories per serving

Takes **35 minutes** + **30 minutes** cooling + freezing + **20 minutes** standing

V

* recommended

1 Heat the milk and vanilla pod in a medium pan until the milk is just boiling. Remove the pan from the heat and whisk in the egg yolks and caster sugar.

2 Using a sieve, strain the mixture into a clean non stick medium saucepan. Mix the cornflour with a little cold water to make a thin paste and add this to the pan. Cook, stirring continuously, until the custard mixture thickens. Cool, remove the vanilla pod, and then chill for 30 minutes.

3 Pour the mixture and yogurt into an ice cream maker, if using, and churn for 20–25 minutes, or according to the manufacturer's instructions. Spoon into a plastic lidded container and place in the freezer for around 4 hours. (If you don't have an ice cream maker, whisk the yogurt into the chilled custard and transfer it to a freezer container, and freeze. After 2 hours remove it from the freezer and whisk well. Freeze for another 2 hours and then whisk again. Return it to the freezer until the ice cream is frozen solid.)

4 About 20 minutes before serving, take the ice cream out of the freezer and let it stand before scooping it out.

Tip When cooling custards, cover with a sheet of dampened greaseproof paper. This will prevent a skin from forming.

Cheesecake Ice Cream

Try this delicious creamy dessert for a special family dinner.

1   Put all the ingredients into a food processor or liquidiser and whisk or blend until thoroughly blended. (You could also do this with an electric whisk.)

2   Pour the mixture into an ice cream maker, if using, and churn for 20–25 minutes, or according to the manufacturer's instructions. Spoon into a plastic lidded container and place in the freezer for around 4 hours. (If you don't have an ice cream maker, pour the whisked mixture into a lidded plastic container and freeze for 1½ hours. Remove from the freezer and stir it through with a fork to remove any lumps. Return it to the freezer for another 1½ hours, then repeat the stirring. Return it to the freezer and leave it for at least 8 hours or preferably overnight).

3   If using an ice cream maker it will be ready to serve after 4 hours. (If not using an ice cream maker, or if not using immediately, remove from the freezer and leave to soften at room temperature for about 20 minutes before serving).

Eat wisely Replace whole or semi-skimmed milk with skimmed milk. There is just as much calcium in skimmed milk as there is in either whole or semi-skimmed, so you can rest assured that your bones won't suffer as a result of the change.

Roly Pavlova

This is a delicious and refreshing dessert the whole family will love.

Serves 8

1 teaspoon vanilla essence
1 teaspoon vinegar
1 teaspoon cornflour
4 egg whites
200 g (7 oz) caster sugar
200 ml (7 fl oz) half fat crème fraîche
500 g (1 lb 2 oz) frozen summer fruits,
 defrosted and drained

 3 POINTS values per serving
24 POINTS values per recipe

C **170 calories** per serving

Takes **20 minutes** to prepare, **45 minutes**
to cook + cooling

V

✳ not recommended

1 Preheat the oven to Gas Mark 2/150°C/fan oven 130°C. Line a 23 x 33 cm (9 x 13 inch) Swiss roll tin with baking parchment.

2 Blend together the vanilla essence, vinegar and cornflour.

3 In a separate grease-free bowl, using a hand-held electric mixer, whisk the egg whites until they form stiff peaks. Whisk in the caster sugar and cornflour mixture in three equal quantities and continue whisking until the mixture is thick and glossy.

4 Spoon the meringue into the prepared tin and level the surface. Bake in the oven for 45 minutes, then turn off the oven. Leave the meringue in the cooling oven for 15 minutes.

5 Turn the meringue out on to a large sheet of greaseproof paper and carefully peel off the baking parchment. Allow to cool completely.

6 Spread the crème fraîche over the meringue and sprinkle with the fruit. Gently roll up from the narrow end, then serve.

Tip Do not worry if the meringue cracks when you roll it up; it adds to its charm.

Variation When soft summer fruits are in season, use them instead of frozen summer berries. Reserve a few for decoration.

Banoffee Pie

A deliciously indulgent low *POINTS* values dessert.

Serves 6

40 g (1½ oz) low fat polyunsaturated margarine
135 g (4¾ oz) reduced fat digestive biscuits, crushed
low fat cooking spray
1 x sachet Angel Delight Butterscotch No Added Sugar
300 ml (10 fl oz) semi skimmed milk
2 bananas, chopped
200 g (7 oz) low fat natural yogurt
3 teaspoons muscovado sugar

4½ *POINTS* values per serving
28 *POINTS* values per recipe

C   288 **calories** per serving

Takes **15 minutes** + **30 minutes** chilling

V

* not recommended

1 Melt the margarine in a small saucepan. Add the crushed biscuits and mix well.

2 Spray a 20 cm (8 inch) loose bottomed flan tin with low fat cooking spray. Pour the crumb mixture into the tin and press it down well, right up to the edges.

3 Leave the flan tin in the fridge for 30 minutes.

4 Make up the butterscotch Angel Delight with the milk according to the sachet instructions. After leaving for 2 minutes, spoon it over the biscuit base and return it to the fridge for 4 minutes or until set.

5 Top with the chopped bananas and then the yogurt.

6 Sprinkle with muscovado sugar and return to the fridge for 2 minutes until the sugar starts to dissolve. Serve the pie cut into six wedges.

Tip The biscuit base can be made well in advance and then you can complete the dessert just before you require it.

Variation Try using different flavours of Angel Delight with different fruits – try strawberry flavour, topped with 150 g (5½ oz) of fresh strawberries, sliced. The *POINTS* values will be the same.

Raspberry Orange Creams

These little desserts are like mini cheesecakes. Serve them with fresh raspberries and an orange and raspberry sauce.

Serves 4

350 g (12 oz) low fat soft cheese
4 tablespoons low fat plain yogurt
1 tablespoon caster sugar
finely grated zest of a lemon
1 tablespoon lemon juice
350 g (12 oz) raspberries
zest and juice of a large orange
artificial sweetener, to taste

1 Put the soft cheese into a bowl and beat with a wooden spoon to soften it. Add the yogurt, caster sugar, lemon zest and lemon juice.

2 Put four individual heart-shaped moulds with drainage holes on to a tray or baking sheet (or use yogurt pots with a couple of holes punched in the base). Spoon the cheese mixture into them, then cover and refrigerate for several hours, or overnight.

3 Reserve half the raspberries, then purée the other half in a blender or liquidiser with the orange juice. Sweeten to taste with the sweetener.

4 Turn out the desserts and serve with the reserved raspberries and the orange and raspberry sauce. Decorate with orange zest.

3 POINTS values per serving
12½ POINTS values per recipe

C **180 calories** per serving

Takes **10 minutes** + several hours chilling

V

✱ not recommended

Tip If you line the pots with dampened butter muslin or new J-cloths (cut to size), you will be able to turn out the desserts easily.

Variation You can serve the desserts in their pots, if you prefer. Just top with the sauce and raspberries, then decorate with orange zest.

Blackberry Meringue Pudding

Here, little pots of blackberries are cooked with cinnamon and mallow meringue. An easy recipe for two, or simply scale the ingredients up for more servings.

Serves 4

30 g (1¼ oz) fresh breadcrumbs
1 teaspoon ground cinnamon
220 g (7½ oz) fresh blackberries
2 egg whites
80 g (3 oz) light muscovado or soft brown sugar

1 Preheat the oven to Gas Mark 5/190°C/fan oven 170°C.

2 Heat a small non stick frying pan over a low heat and dry fry the breadcrumbs and cinnamon, stirring occasionally, until toasted and crisp. Remove from the heat and fold through the blackberries.

3 In a small grease-free bowl, whisk the egg white to stiff peaks. Whisk in half the sugar and then fold in the remainder. Fold the blackberry mixture through the meringue and divide between four 8 cm (3¼ inch) ramekin dishes. Bake for 15 minutes until golden.

 2 POINTS values per serving
9 POINTS values per recipe

C **116 calories** per serving

Takes **10 minutes** to prepare,
15 minutes to cook

V

✱ not recommended

Variation Replace some of the blackberries with redcurrants or blueberries, or all the fruits with fresh raspberries. The **POINTS** values will remain the same.

Quick Fruit Crumble

This simple and satisfying dessert is assembled in no time using a can of fruit and a quickly whizzed up crumble topping – just right for a midweek pudding. Serve with 1 tablespoon low fat natural yogurt, for an extra ½ **POINTS** value per serving.

Serves 4

1 x 420 g can peaches in natural juice, drained
1 ripe banana, sliced thinly
50 g (1¾ oz) low fat polyunsaturated margarine
100 g (3½ oz) plain white flour
1 tablespoon light soft brown sugar
2 tablespoons porridge oats
freshly grated nutmeg

 4½ POINTS values per serving
17 POINTS values per recipe

C **240 calories** per serving

Takes **10 minutes** to prepare,
20 minutes to cook

V

✳ not recommended

1 Preheat the oven to Gas Mark 5/190°C/fan oven 170°C.

2 Tip the canned fruit into a medium size baking dish – chop the fruit if necessary. Mix in the banana slices.

3 Place the margarine, flour and sugar in a food processor and whizz until the mixture resembles fine breadcrumbs. Stir in the porridge oats. Spoon this topping over the fruit and sprinkle over nutmeg.

4 Place the dish on a baking tray and bake in the oven for 20 minutes until the topping is lightly browned.

Variation In spring, try 400 g (14 oz) tender, pink forced rhubarb instead of the peaches. There's no need to precook it. Chop it and add 1 tablespoon of caster sugar, for 4 **POINTS** values per serving.

Rhubarb Crumble

Serve this old favourite hot with 1 tablespoon of virtually fat free fromage frais, for an extra ½ **POINTS** value per serving.

Serves 6

1 kg (2 lb 4 oz) rhubarb, trimmed and cut into small pieces
3 tablespoons artificial sweetener
100 g (3½ oz) plain white or wholemeal flour
100 g (3½ oz) porridge oats
50 g (1¾ oz) demerara sugar
1 teaspoon ground cinnamon
50 g (1¾ oz) low fat polyunsaturated margarine, straight from the fridge

1 Preheat the oven to Gas Mark 6/200°C/fan oven 180°C. Place the rhubarb in a saucepan with 200 ml (7 fl oz) water and the sweetener. Cover and simmer for 10 minutes until soft then pour into a 1.2 litre (2 pint) ovenproof dish.

2 Put the flour, oats, demerara sugar and cinnamon in a food processor. Cut the margarine into pieces and add to the dry mixture. Pulse to make a coarse blend.

3 Sprinkle the crumble mixture over the rhubarb and bake for 20–30 minutes, until pale golden and the fruit bubbles up at the edges.

3 POINTS values per serving
17 POINTS values per recipe

C **193 calories** per serving

Takes **10 minutes** to prepare, **30 minutes** to bake

V

 ✱ not recommended

Variation This could also be made with canned rhubarb or with fresh gooseberries, apricots, plums, apples or pears.

Cherry and Almond Omelette

Cherries and almonds conjure up memories of Italy with its lovely fruit orchards.

Serves 6

25 g (1 oz) butter
2 x 425 g cans pitted black cherries, drained
4 eggs, beaten
100 g (3½ oz) low fat natural fromage frais
25 g (1 oz) caster sugar
25 g (1 oz) ground almonds
15 g (½ oz) flaked almonds
a dusting of icing sugar

1 Melt the butter in a large heavy-based frying pan. (The handle needs to be able to withstand the heat of the grill). Heat the cherries in the butter for 3–4 minutes or until slightly softened.

2 Beat together the eggs, fromage frais, sugar and ground almonds. Pour over the cherries. Stir for 3–4 minutes, then leave to lightly set for a further 5 minutes.

3 Sprinkle the flaked almonds over the top and place under a grill preheated to medium, to lightly toast the nuts. Serve warm, dusted with icing sugar.

4½ POINTS values per serving
28 POINTS values per recipe

C **230 calories** per serving

Takes **25 minutes**

V

✳ not recommended

Variation Serve with a 60 g (2 oz) scoop of low fat vanilla ice cream, for an extra 1 *POINTS* value per serving.

Apple Pie

Always a favourite with family and friends, this apple pie is packed with flavour and is delicious served hot or cold.

Serves 6

low fat cooking spray
700 g (1 lb 9 oz) cooking apples, peeled, cored and quartered
2 tablespoons honey
50 g (1¾ oz) caster sugar
1 tablespoon cornflour
2 teaspoons cinnamon
juice and zest of a lemon
½ teaspoon vanilla essence

For the pastry

75 g (2¾ oz) plain flour, seasoned with ½ teaspoon salt
50 g (1¾ oz) low fat polyunsaturated margarine
a little skimmed milk, to glaze

 3 *POINTS* values per serving
17½ *POINTS* values per recipe

C   176 **calories** per serving

⊘ Takes **25 minutes** to prepare + cooling, **30 minutes** to cook

V

✱ recommended

1 Preheat the oven to Gas Mark 5/190°C/fan oven 170°C and spray a 20 cm (8 inch) pie dish with the low fat cooking spray.

2 Make the pastry by mixing together 1 tablespoon of the flour, the margarine and 2 teaspoons of water with a fork. Then add the rest of the flour and mix together. Turn out on to a floured board and knead lightly just until it comes together into a ball. Put in a plastic bag and refrigerate until needed.

3 Put the apples in a lidded pan with 4 tablespoons of water, cover and simmer gently for 10 minutes until the apples are beginning to soften. Add the honey, sugar, cornflour, cinnamon, lemon juice, zest and vanilla and stir until thick. Leave to cool slightly.

4 Roll out the pastry to fit the top of the dish with a little to spare. Put the apple in the dish and cover with the pastry. Press the edges down on top of the sides of the dish and cut off any excess. Make short slashes in the centre with a knife to allow the steam to escape and decorate with the pastry trimmings cut into leaf shapes.

5 Brush the pastry with a little skimmed milk and bake for 30 minutes or until the pastry is golden and crisp.

Eat wisely Replace butter, which is high in saturated fat, with low fat polyunsaturated margarine.

Lemon Meringue Pie

This is a simply delicious low *POINTS* version of the traditional favourite.

Serves 4

For the pastry
150 g (5½ oz) plain flour
a pinch of salt
75 g (2¾ oz) low fat polyunsaturated
  margarine

For the filling
3 tablespoons cornflour
150 ml (5 fl oz) water
juice and grated zest of 2 lemons
50 g (1¾ oz) caster sugar

For the meringue
2 egg whites
50 g (1¾ oz) caster sugar

5 *POINTS* values per serving
19½ *POINTS* values per recipe

341 **calories** per serving

Takes **30 minutes** to prepare + **30 minutes** chilling, **30 minutes** to cook

V

✱ recommended (base only)

1 To make the pastry, mix the flour and salt together. Rub in the margarine until the mixture resembles breadcrumbs.

2 Sprinkle over 1–2 tablespoons water and mix with a palette knife until the pastry comes together into lumps. Draw it together quickly with your hand, wrap in cling film and place in the refrigerator for at least 30 minutes.

3 Preheat the oven to Gas Mark 7/220°C/fan oven 200°C. On a floured surface, roll out the dough to fit a shallow 20 cm (8 inch) tart tin. Prick all over with a fork and line with foil or baking paper and scatter with baking beans (ordinary dried beans will do). Bake for 15 minutes.

4 Remove the beans and foil or paper and bake for a further 5 minutes.

5 Mix the cornflour with the water in a saucepan. Add the lemon juice and zest and bring to the boil, stirring, until the mixture thickens. Add the sugar and stir.

6 Pour the filling into the pastry case and make the meringue. In a clean grease-free bowl, whisk the egg whites until they are stiff then whisk in half the sugar. Fold in the rest of the sugar and then pile the meringue on top of the lemon mixture.

7 Bake for 10 minutes or until the meringue is crisp and lightly browned. Leave to cool before serving or the centre will be runny.

Variation For Key Lime Pie, follow the same recipe but use limes instead of the lemons.

Lemon and Ginger Tart

This is a soft-setting tart, rather than a firmly set one like a cheesecake. Try it, it is absolutely delicious.

Serves 6

25 g (1 oz) low fat polyunsaturated
  margarine
10 reduced fat ginger snap biscuits, crushed
2 large lemons, preferably unwaxed
1 x 405 g can skimmed, light condensed milk

3 *POINTS* values per serving
17 *POINTS* values per recipe

281 calories per serving

Takes **15 minutes** + chilling

V

✳ not recommended

1 Melt the margarine in a pan over a low heat. Add the crushed ginger snaps and 1 tablespoon of water and mix well. Press into a 20 cm (8 inch) pie dish. Chill until required.

2 Finely grate the zest of both lemons. Squeeze the juice from one lemon and half of the other, reserving the remaining half lemon to slice. Mix the juice into the condensed milk, which will thicken almost immediately, and then spoon over the biscuit base. Smooth the surface and chill for at least 1 hour until softly set.

3 Thinly slice the remaining lemon and use to decorate the tart.

Eat wisely Subtle changes in your usual eating habits can make a big difference to the way that you feel. Make gradual adjustments like reducing the amount of processed foods you eat.

Hot Chocolate Cake

Indulge your passion for chocolate with this delicious recipe that the whole family will love.

Serves 4

55 g (2 oz) low fat polyunsaturated
   margarine
55 g (2 oz) caster sugar
1 egg
40 g (1½ oz) self raising flour
15 g (½ oz) cocoa powder

3 **POINTS** values per serving
11½ **POINTS** values per recipe

C 170 calories per serving

Takes 10 minutes

V

✱ recommended

1 Cream together the margarine and sugar in a 1.2 litre (2 pint) pudding basin.

2 Beat in the egg and then carefully fold in the flour and cocoa powder.

3 Mix well and then microwave on high for 2 minutes.

4 Allow to stand for 3–4 minutes, then turn out and serve immediately.

Cooking basics Eggs are a versatile, high protein food and indispensable in the kitchen. Always bring eggs up to room temperature before using, as a cold egg won't whisk well and the shell will crack if placed in hot water.

Black Forest Trifle Cake

This recipe is a bit of a cross between a tiramisu and a Black Forest gâteau. Needless to say, it is utterly delicious but it is also very quick and easy to make, too.

Serves 6

24 sponge fingers
2 x 400 g cans stoned cherries, drained, 6 tablespoons of juice reserved
2 tablespoons kirsch or brandy (optional)
200 g (7 oz) very low fat fromage frais
150 g (5½ oz) Quark
50 g (1¾ oz) icing sugar
1 teaspoon vanilla essence
1 teaspoon cocoa powder, to dust

4 POINTS values per serving
23½ POINTS values per recipe

259 calories per serving

Takes **25 minutes** to prepare
+ **30 minutes** chilling

V

✳ not recommended

1 Line the base and sides of a 900 g (2 lb) loaf tin with clingfilm, allowing extra to hang over the sides. Place a layer of eight sponge fingers in the bottom, sugar side down, and then arrange half the cherries on top and sprinkle with half the reserved cherry juice and 1 tablespoon of the kirsch or brandy, if using.

2 Beat half of the fromage frais with the Quark, sugar and vanilla essence until smooth. Spread half of this mixture over the cherries. Then arrange another layer of sponge fingers on top. Repeat with the remaining cherries, juice and cheese mixture, finishing with a layer of sponge fingers.

3 Fold the clingfilm over the top and press down with your fingers; then chill for at least 30 minutes.

4 Turn out on to a serving plate and remove the clingfilm. Spread the top with the remaining fromage frais and dust with cocoa powder.

Summer Puddings

In these individual summer puddings, the bread is layered in small pudding basins to make them easy to assemble – and they look so attractive when turned out.

Serves 2

75 g (2¾ oz) redcurrants or blackcurrants
75 g (2¾ oz) blueberries
1 tablespoon caster sugar
75 g (2¾ oz) strawberries, sliced
75 g (2¾ oz) raspberries
3 medium slices white bread

To serve
2 tablespoons very low fat natural
    fromage frais
a few mint leaves

3½ *POINTS* values per serving
7 *POINTS* values per recipe

C   190 calories per serving

Takes 20 minutes
    + several hours chilling

V

* recommended

1 Reserve two sprigs of redcurrants or blackcurrants and put the remainder in a medium saucepan with the blueberries and sugar. Heat gently until the juice just begins to run – about 2–3 minutes. Remove from the heat and stir in the strawberries and raspberries. Leave to cool.

2 Use biscuit cutters to stamp out circles from the slices of bread to fit into two individual pudding basins. You will need two 5 cm (2 inch) circles, two 6 cm (2½ inch) circles and two 7.5 cm (2¾ inch) circles.

3 Pop the smallest bread circles in the base of each pudding basin. Using a draining spoon (slotted spoon), divide half the fruit mixture between the basins. Place a medium-sized bread circle on top of each and then spoon in the rest of the fruit, reserving some of the juice. Finish with the largest circles of bread, pressing each down well.

4 Spoon a little remaining fruit juice over the bread and then place clingfilm tightly over. Place a weight on top of each basin. Refrigerate for several hours, or overnight if you prefer.

5 To serve, run a knife around the inside of each basin, and turn the puddings out on to individual plates. Serve each one with a tablespoon of fromage frais and decorate with mint leaves and the reserved fruit sprigs.

Tips Whizz the leftover bread in a blender or food processor to make breadcrumbs, pack in a polythene bag and refrigerate or freeze to use in another recipe.

Try using defrosted frozen summer berries in this recipe – there's no need for any cooking, as they are already soft.

Chocolate Profiteroles

Discover the miracle of low *POINTS* value profiteroles.

Serves 4 (Makes 12)

25 g (1 oz) low fat polyunsaturated margarine
75 g (2¾ oz) plain flour
a pinch of salt
1 egg
1 egg yolk
1 x 500 g tub 0% fat Greek style yogurt
2 teaspoons vanilla essence
1 tablespoon clear honey
2 tablespoons cornflour
2 tablespoons low fat drinking chocolate
300 ml (10 fl oz) skimmed milk

4 *POINTS* values per serving
17 *POINTS* values per recipe

C **300 calories** per serving

Takes **25 minutes** to prepare,
20 minutes to cook

V

✳ not recommended

1 Preheat the oven to Gas Mark 6/200°C/fan oven 180°C and line a baking sheet with non stick baking parchment.

2 Heat the margarine and 150 ml (5 fl oz) water together in a large saucepan until the margarine has just melted. Meanwhile, put the flour on to a piece of baking paper with the salt and mix together.

3 Take the saucepan off the heat and, working quickly, add all the flour mix into the pan using the baking paper as a funnel. Beat together with a wooden spoon for at least 1 minute until well blended and the mixture comes away from the side of the pan in one lump.

4 Allow to cool for 10 minutes. Beat together the whole egg and the egg yolk and add to the cooled mixture, half at a time. Beat with a wooden spoon until the mixture is smooth, thick and glossy – this is quite hard. Place 12 heaped teaspoons well apart on the baking tray.

5 Bake for 15–20 minutes until well risen and golden. Remove from the oven and, with a sharp knife, slit each profiterole to let the air out. Place back in the turned off oven, the door slightly ajar so they dry out inside and cool.

6 Mix together the yogurt, vanilla and honey. Spoon into the cool profiteroles. Pile them up on a serving plate.

7 Blend the cornflour and drinking chocolate with a little of the milk in a saucepan. Blend in the rest of the milk, bring to the boil, stirring all the time, until thickened and smooth. Pour over the profiteroles to serve.

Bread and Peach Pudding

A unique and very tasty version of a much loved classic.

Serves 4

low fat cooking spray
3 thick slices brown bread
1 x 410 g (14¼ oz) canned peaches in juice
2 tablespoons mixed dried fruit
200 ml (7 fl oz) semi skimmed milk
2 eggs, beaten
½ teaspoon ground nutmeg
2 teaspoons muscovado sugar

 3½ **POINTS** values per serving
13 **POINTS** values per recipe

C 210 **calories** per serving

Takes **15 minutes** to prepare,
40 minutes to cook

V

✱ not recommended

1 Preheat the oven to Gas Mark 4/180°C/fan oven 160°C.

2 Spray a medium size shallow ovenproof dish with low fat cooking spray.

3 Break up the slices of bread and place them in the dish.

4 Drain the peaches, reserving the juice and chop them roughly. Place them in the dish with the bread. Sprinkle over the mixed dried fruit.

5 Whisk together the reserved juice, milk and eggs and pour this over the bread and fruit.

6 Sprinkle the top with the nutmeg and muscovado sugar and bake in the oven for 40 minutes, until golden.

Variation Most fruits work well in this recipe – try tinned pears or apricots for a change. The **POINTS** values will remain the same.

Rhubarb and Orange Fool

A fruit-flavoured fromage frais lends a lot more flavour to this easy dessert.

Serves 6

350 g (12 oz) rhubarb, trimmed and cut
  into chunks
finely grated zest and juice of an orange
50 g (1¾ oz) fructose
1 x 150 ml (5 fl oz) pot low fat
  ready-to-serve custard
1 x 11 g sachet gelatine
1 x 200 g (7 oz) tub orange flavour
  fromage frais
1 egg white

 2 POINTS values per serving
11½ POINTS values per recipe

C **80 calories** per serving

Takes **20 minutes** + cooling
+ **2 hours** chilling

V

✳ not recommended

1 Place the rhubarb in a saucepan with the orange zest, juice and fructose. Cook over a gentle heat until the rhubarb is pulpy and then remove from the heat. Allow to cool.

2 When cool, transfer to a food processor with the custard and blend until smooth.

3 Place 3 tablespoons of water in a small heatproof dish and sprinkle the gelatine over. Allow to stand for 5 minutes, until it looks spongy. Then heat gently over a pan of simmering water until the gelatine dissolves. Add to the food processor and blend for a couple of seconds.

4 Pour the rhubarb mixture into a mixing bowl and stir in the fromage frais. In a clean, grease-free bowl, whisk the egg white until it forms soft peaks and fold into the rhubarb mixture. Transfer to six individual glasses and chill for at least 2 hours before serving.

Tip You'll find fructose in the supermarket next to the sugar.

Variation Try using strawberry or peach-flavoured fromage frais for a change, for the same **POINTS** values.

Fruity Chocolate Fridge Cake

Serves 8

110 g (4 oz) plain chocolate (at least 70% cocoa solids)

50 g (1¾ oz) low fat polyunsaturated margarine

2 egg whites

125 g (4½ oz) low fat digestive biscuits, crushed roughly

75 g (2¾ oz) ready to eat dried apricots, chopped

3½ **POINTS** values per serving
29 **POINTS** values per recipe

C 192 **calories** per serving

Takes **15 minutes** + **2 hours** chilling

V

* not recommended

1 Place the chocolate and margarine in a heatproof bowl. Bring a small pan of water to simmer, rest the bowl over the pan and stir to melt. Alternatively, melt the chocolate and margarine in a microwave. Set aside to cool slightly.

2 Meanwhile, in a clean grease-free bowl, whisk the egg whites until they form stiff peaks. Carefully fold the whites into the chocolate mixture followed by the biscuits and apricots, reserving a few of the chopped apricots to decorate the top.

3 Spread the mixture over the base of a loose bottomed 20 cm (8 inch) pie tin and decorate with the reserved apricots. Chill for at least 2 hours before cutting into wedges.

Chocolate Roulade

Serves 6

low fat cooking spray
75 g (2¾ oz) plain white flour
2 tablespoons unsweetened cocoa powder
3 large eggs
75 g (2¾ oz) unrefined caster sugar
200 g (7 oz) low fat soft cheese
100 ml (3½ fl oz) very low fat raspberry
 fromage frais
100 g (3½ oz) raspberries, defrosted if frozen
2 teaspoons icing sugar, for dusting
a few mint leaves, to decorate

1 Preheat the oven to Gas Mark 7/220°C/fan oven 200°C. Spray a 18 x 28 cm (7 x 11 inch) Swiss roll tin with low fat cooking spray and line it with greaseproof paper. Spray the paper with low fat cooking spray.

2 Sift the flour and cocoa powder into a bowl. Set aside. Break the eggs into a large mixing bowl and add the caster sugar. Use a hand held electric mixer, whisk them together until very light and pale in colour. This will take about 5 minutes.

3 Sift the flour and cocoa mixture again, this time into the egg mixture. Fold it in gently using a large metal spoon, not a wooden one. Pour the mixture into the prepared tin and spread it out to the corners.

4 Bake in the oven for 7–9 minutes, until firm yet springy when you touch it. Turn it out on to a large sheet of greaseproof paper, and then carefully peel away the lining paper. Cover with a clean, damp tea towel and leave the sponge until cold.

5 Mix together the soft cheese and fromage frais. Reserve a few raspberries for decoration, and then lightly mash the remainder with a fork. Stir these into the soft cheese mixture.

6 Trim the edges of the chocolate sponge, fill with the raspberry mixture and roll it up. Sprinkle with icing sugar and serve, decorated with mint leaves and the reserved raspberries.

3½ *POINTS* values per serving
22 *POINTS* values per recipe

C   220 calories per serving

Takes 30 minutes

V

* recommended

Variation To make a Peach Melba Roulade, omit the cocoa powder from the mixture and use a peach or raspberry flavoured fromage frais, and add a chopped peach to the filling. The *POINTS* values per serving will remain the same.

Strawberry and Hazelnut Strata

Serves 4

40 g (1½ oz) fresh breadcrumbs
25 g (1 oz) demerara sugar
15 g (½ oz) chopped hazelnuts
300 g (10½ oz) strawberries, sliced
1 tablespoon icing sugar
1 x 500 g carton low fat custard, chilled

1. Preheat the oven to Gas Mark 4/180°C/fan oven 160°C.

2. Mix the breadcrumbs with the sugar and hazelnuts and spread out on a tray lined with baking parchment.

3. Bake for 8 minutes, stirring halfway through, until the crumbs are caramelised and crisp. Cool.

4. Mix the strawberries with the icing sugar to sweeten.

5. Layer the chilled custard, strawberries and crunchy hazelnut crumbs into four dessert glasses or bowls. Serve immediately.

3 POINTS values per serving
13 POINTS values per recipe

191 calories per serving

Takes **10 minutes** to prepare,
8 minutes to cook + cooling

V

* not recommended

Index